A SCENIC
Georgia Sketchbook

A SCENIC
Georgia Sketchbook

*Landmarks & Wonders
from the Back Roads*

Ronald R. Huffman

THE History PRESS

Published by The History Press
Charleston, SC
www.historypress.com

Copyright © 2021 by Ronald R. Huffman
All rights reserved

First published 2021

Manufactured in the United States

ISBN 9781467149402

Library of Congress Control Number applied for.

Notice: The information in this book is true and complete to the best of our knowledge. It is offered without guarantee on the part of the author or The History Press. The author and The History Press disclaim all liability in connection with the use of this book.

All rights reserved. No part of this book may be reproduced or transmitted in any form whatsoever without prior written permission from the publisher except in the case of brief quotations embodied in critical articles and reviews.

CONTENTS

Preface	7
Introduction	9
1. Metropolitan Atlanta	11
2. South Georgia	61
3. Central Georgia	83
4. North Georgia	109
Acknowledgements	133
Appendix A. The Seven Natural Wonders of Georgia	137
Appendix B. Georgia During the Civil War	139
Appendix C. Outline of Georgia History to 1861	143
Appendix D. Georgia's Capital Cities	147
Appendix E. Sketch Locator	149
Bibliography	151
About the Author	155

PREFACE

The idea for this book germinated in the summer of 1982 when I was interning for a small firm in Montgomery, Alabama. My first task was to design a decorative perimeter brick wall for a residence in town. My boss at the time asked me to design and detail the wall, and he would return later in the day to review my work. Unfortunately, I spent the entire time struggling with wall construction. I focused on rebar, concrete block, the number of brick courses, the footing depth and the size of the piers. I completely ignored the actual look of the wall. Upon his return, my boss very nicely asked me to grab my sketchbook and follow him. We jumped into his convertible and drove around historic areas in Montgomery. We stopped along the way whenever there was an interesting brick wall. He asked me to sketch each wall. After a couple of hours or so he pulled over and asked me if I had seen enough to design a nice brick wall. Together we quickly sketched the fundamental character of what eventually became a beautiful wall. At that time, I thought that a sketchbook on walls, fences and gates would be a fun and unique book.

In many ways, this book represents a lifetime of fun, but I had several goals in mind in developing this book. Initially, the book was planned to simply be a compilation of my sketches of fences and walls. However, I kept finding other, more interesting sketch material. I expanded the idea to include the unique places I have had the pleasure to visit and sketch around Georgia. There is no logic to what I sketch. I simply see something that I like, often an obscure or forgotten piece of roadside architecture

Preface

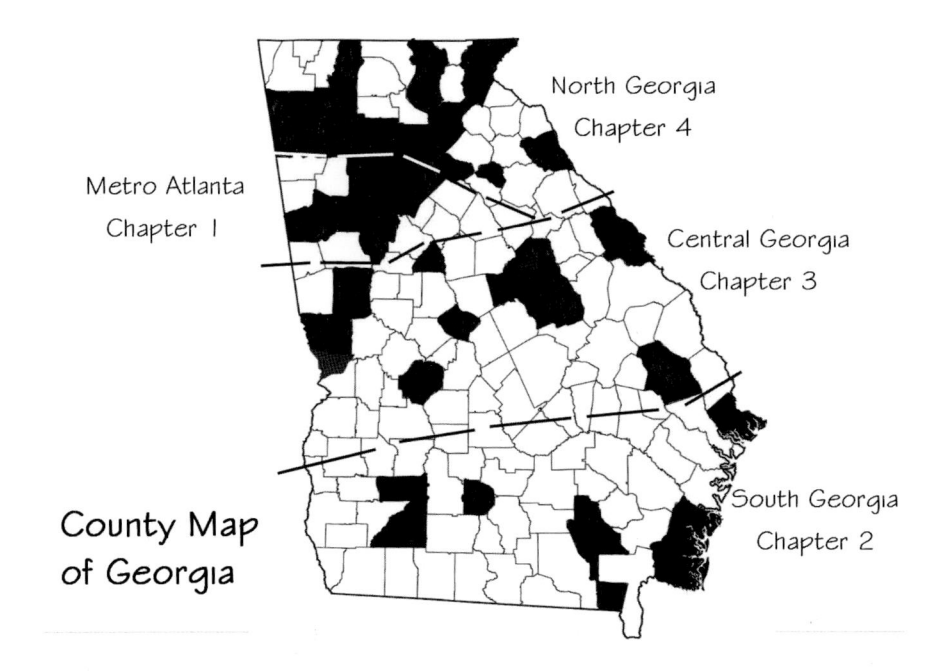

County Map of Georgia

- Metro Atlanta — Chapter 1
- North Georgia — Chapter 4
- Central Georgia — Chapter 3
- South Georgia — Chapter 2

and stop to photograph and sketch. As I assembled the sketches for the book, I concluded it would be best to organize the sketches based on the prominent physiographic regions in the state such as the Coastal Plain, the Fall Line, Metro Atlanta and North Georgia.

All of the sketches are in Georgia. The sketches are untouched and unedited (no Photoshop). Because the sketches are presented in their original state, the reproduction is not always clear and crisp. Most of the sketches were drawn on vellum, but some were drawn on thin yellow and white trace paper that is commonly used by architects. Some of the sketches are more than thirty years old and did not scan as well as I had hoped. I am hoping that part of the fun is to see the sketches in the raw form that they were drawn.

The general location either city or county is noted for each sketch. I tried to be geographically diverse in my selected offering but was restricted to the places I have traveled to or through in the last thirty-five years around Georgia. Hopefully the reader will enjoy my interpretation of historic and roadside Georgia and maybe look at similar places in their own community in a new way. Thanks for looking.

INTRODUCTION

I have always admired finely crafted, historic architectural drawings. Early in my career, I worked for an architectural and engineering company that had gone into business in 1917 and had a basement full of drawings dating back to that time. I always enjoyed looking over the old "linen" drawings and admired the incredible attention to detail. I realize that with the advent of computer-aided drafting and design, these types of beautifully crafted drawings are disappearing along with the ability to create them. As the world of computer technology speeds up our delivery of products and services, I thought I would focus on reintroducing the craft through my drawings and sketches. I began including pencil sketches with my project plans as a way to add extra value to the work we were producing for our clients in the 1980s. I have noticed since that time that my clients appreciate the attention to detail and realize that the work represents my personal commitment to them and their projects.

The content of each chapter focuses on unique local historic buildings, roadside architecture and obscure historic places around the state. Quite a few sketches are included that feature the fine details that I have long admired in historic brick, stone and woodwork on old buildings, fences and walls. I also have long admired the unique gateways found around the state and the spectacular clock towers found on our beautiful flagship university campuses.

Chapter 1 includes sketches of places around Metropolitan Atlanta. I raised my family in Cobb County, and my professional office is in Atlanta.

Introduction

I tried not including too many sketches from the metro area, but I have lived and worked there for thirty-five years.

Chapters 2 through 4 represent different regions around the state. I have been lucky to be able to spend much of my career providing design and planning services to small towns and counties around Georgia. My practice has enabled me to travel to all corners of the state. The sketches in these chapters are of many of the unique and wonderful places that can be found around Georgia. Chapter 2 captures places found in Georgia's Coastal Plain areas from Waycross and Savannah in the southeast to Albany in the southwest. Chapter 3 includes places in and around the fall line such as Augusta, Macon and Columbus but even includes places such as Sandersville and Sparta. Chapter 4 features places in North Georgia, including fun locations such as Brasstown Bald, the Dahlonega Gold Museum and the Richard B. Russell Dam.

I
METROPOLITAN ATLANTA

The whole world is a painting…well you know, everything in it.
—*Raymond Huffman, age ten*

I moved to the Atlanta area in 1986 and settled in Cobb County. Since 1986, I have witnessed the growth of Atlanta from a metropolis of around 1.5 million people to an international city with a metropolitan population approaching 6 million. During the last thirty-three years, I have seen rapid growth and development threaten historic properties across the region. As a result, I developed an appreciation for historic properties and roadside landmarks simply because of their uniqueness in the face of the rampant growth.

Many of my sketches are of places in Cobb County, including the cities of Marietta and Acworth. However, the Atlanta metropolitan area is huge and, for the purposes of this book, includes communities as far north as Milton in Fulton County, Cartersville in Bartow County, Douglas County to the west, Fayette and Clayton County to the south and DeKalb County to the east.

By far, my favorite part of the region is the area around the Concord Road Covered Bridge in Cobb County. The Covered Bridge Historic District is rich in pre–Civil War and Civil War history. Other unique and wonderful treasures can be found around the Marietta Square, in Decatur near Agnes Scott College and in Roswell around the mills and the town square. One of the most beautiful spots in the region can be found at Starr's Mill in Fayette County. In downtown Atlanta, Joel Chandler Harris's house is an absolute architectural treasure, and Oakland Cemetery is rich in architectural details, sculpture, specimen trees and history.

I live near the Concord Road Covered Bridge and enjoy taking out-of-town guests to see the nearby historic sites, including the Covered Bridge, the Mable House and the Silver Comet Trail. I also always enjoy taking guests to the Marietta Square for the restaurants and art galleries. If we have out-of-town guests looking for the antebellum South, then I usually head over to Roswell for a tour of Bulloch Hall and Barrington Hall. For friends and family looking for more of an urban experience, I usually steer the activities to include a trip to Centennial Olympic Park and the Coca-Cola Museum.

Project Notes

Even though I have worked on many terrific projects all over the state, I have identified a few of my favorite projects in every region. In the Atlanta metropolitan area, the majority of my work has been within Cobb County. I have had the opportunity to work for the county as well as the Cities of Marietta, Kennesaw and Acworth. In Cobb County, I was responsible for the design and planning of quite a few parks, including portions of Lost Mountain Park, Tramore Park, Harrison Park, Noonday Creek Park, Hyde Farm, the Heritage Park and the Mable House Amphitheater. By far, my favorite of those projects was the design and eventual construction of the Heritage Park located along Nickajack Creek, including the Concord Road Covered Bridge.

My firm was initially hired by the Cobb Land Trust to master plan the lands assembled and surrounding the future East–West Connector road corridor as it passed through the Covered Bridge Historic District. The project was unusually challenging because the road had not been built yet. We had to determine the boundaries of the park and plan facilities around the road corridor that we could not see on the ground. At that time, there was an abandoned railroad corridor that passed through the future parkland; it eventually became the Silver Comet Trail. The park design considered the abandoned railroad, as well as historic resources such as the Covered Bridge, the Woolen Mill ruins and Civil War earthworks. The future park was also bisected by Nick-a-jack Creek.

We prepared the master plan in 1996 as Atlanta was preparing for the Olympics. The vision for the park included capturing the historic as well as the natural resources in the design themes. We planned for two interpretive centers to be located on opposite ends of the linear park. We planned a nature center at the intersection of Fontaine Road and Nick-a-jack Road, and we planned a heritage center at the end of Fowler Road. The nature center was built, and the heritage center was not. From the beginning, we decided to design the buildings and pavilions with the use of heavy beams and natural stone. To me, the Heritage Park Nature Center is one of the nicest buildings in the Cobb County Park system. At that time, we also did the initial planning and construction of the first section of the Silver Comet Trail. I hosted a series of public meetings and heard countless complaints about the future trail idea. Most people thought it would lead to crime and other illicit activities. Of course, today the trail is embraced and promoted as a major asset in the region.

My other favorite projects in the region include the master planning and design of the Barnes-Mable House Amphitheater. I met Governor Roy Barnes and was honored to design the amphitheater that bears his name. I have also worked with the City of Acworth for more than twenty years in the revitalization of its downtown, including designing a new railroad pedestrian bridge and depot visitor's center.

List of Illustrations

1. Concord Road Covered Bridge, Cobb County
2. Gristmill, Cobb County
3. Gazebo on the Marietta Square, Marietta, Cobb County
4. Marietta National Cemetery, Marietta, Cobb County
5. Brumby Hall, Marietta, Cobb County
6. Texaco Sign, Old Dixie Highway, Acworth, Cobb County
7. A.J. White's Service Station, Old Dixie Highway, Cobb County
8. Rosenwald School, Acworth, Cobb County
9. The Well at Hyde Farm, Cobb County
10. The Barn at Hyde Farm, Cobb County
11. Kennesaw Mountain National Battlefield, Cobb County
12. Sweet Potato Barn, Mable House, Mableton, Cobb County
13. Baptist Student Union, Georgia State University, Atlanta, Fulton County
14. The Swan House, Atlanta, Fulton County
15. Tech Tower, Georgia Institute of Technology, Atlanta, Fulton County

16. Bobby Jones Golf Course, Atlanta, Fulton County
17. The Wren's Nest, Home of Joel Chandler Harris, Atlanta, Fulton County
18. Big Bethel AME Church, Auburn Avenue, Atlanta, Fulton County
19. Five Points, Atlanta, Fulton County
20. Oakland Cemetery, Atlanta, Fulton County
21. Gateway Monument, Buckhead, Atlanta, Fulton County
22. Bulloch Hall, Roswell, Fulton County
23. Agnes Scott College, McCain Entrance, Decatur, DeKalb County
24. Main Gate at Emory University, Decatur, DeKalb County
25. Old Campbell County Courthouse, Fairburn, Fulton County
26. Dillard's Hardware Store, Fairburn, Fulton County
27. Downtown Fairburn, Fulton County
28. Quarters 10, Fort McPherson, Atlanta, Fulton County
29. Guardhouse, Fort McPherson, Atlanta, Fulton County
30. Confederate Monument, Douglasville, Douglas County
31. Starr's Mill, Fayette County
32. Administration Building, Fort Gillem, Clayton County
33. Wick's Tavern, Villa Rica, Carroll County
34. Tenant House at McDaniel Farm Park, Duluth, Gwinnett County
35. The Root House, Marietta, Cobb County

Concord Road Covered Bridge, Cobb County

The original Concord Road Bridge over Nickajack Creek was probably built in the 1840s and is credited to an early Cobb County pioneer, Robert Daniell. During the Civil War, it was burned. Various replacement bridges have been washed out or swept away in flash floods. The present-day bridge appearance probably dates from 1891 and is credited to John Wesley Ruff. The bridge is one of seventeen covered bridges remaining in Georgia. It is still used and open to daily automobile traffic. The covered bridge is now the centerpiece of the Covered Bridge Historic District, which was created by Cobb County in 1986.

The primary reason bridges were covered was to protect the structure from the weather. Effects of rain, snow, ice and sun would accelerate deterioration of wooden bridges. Rain, snow and ice could also make a bridge slippery. Another reason to cover a bridge was to help get livestock that would otherwise be hesitant at the sight of flowing water to cross.

I first sketched this covered bridge in 1996 as part of the master plan I was preparing for the Heritage Park. The park was planned and built as part of a mitigation strategy to compensate for effects from the construction of a new parkway through the Covered Bridge Historic District. Years later, I bought a house nearby and frequently go for walks to and through the bridge with my wife. It has become a symbol of my sketching style and the reason I selected it first in this chapter and for use on the cover of the book.

Gristmill, Cobb County

The Daniell and Ruff's Mill (originally owned and operated by Robert Daniell and Lacy H. Griffith) was built in the late 1840s as a gristmill for grinding corn and making flour. Lacy Griffith sold his half interest in the mill to Martin L. Ruff in 1856. It functioned as a gristmill until the late 1920s, when the mill works were moved to another location. It had an overshot wheel on the north side fed by a millrace carrying water from an upstream dam. It is located adjacent to the Concord Covered Bridge and overlooks Nickajack Creek. On July 4, 1864, the Battle of Ruff's Mill occurred nearby as Union troops advanced against the Confederate line defending the crossing at the covered bridge during the Campaign for Atlanta. It is probable that pockmarks in the stucco may have been due to bullets ricocheting during the battle. The gristmill is depicted on battle maps prepared by Sherman's engineers as part of the Battle for Atlanta in 1864.

My next-door neighbor (David Daniell) is a descendant of the Daniell associated with the old mill. I sketched the mill as a gift for my neighbors at Christmas. It is very difficult to get a good view of the mill. It sits back off the road on the banks of Nickajack Creek. I had to hike along an unmarked trail along the creek to find the view I wanted to capture the unique building. Built with stone and wood, the building remains relatively unchanged since it was erected more than 150 years ago.

The mill and the covered bridge are part of a historic district that also includes the John Gann House, the Concord Woolen Mill ruins, the Henry Clay Ruff House, the John Rice House and the Martin Luker Ruff House. The mill and the adjacent miller's house are listed in the National Register of Historic Places.

Gazebo on the Marietta Square, Marietta, Cobb County

The Marietta Square is one of the finest squares you can find anywhere in Georgia. It has become a thriving hub of activity with great surrounding restaurants and shops. The square has hosted a wide range of activities, including art shows, farmers markets, a skating rink and Santa. The square can be found on almost every old map of the city.

    The Cobb County courthouse that used to occupy the square burned in 1848. Mayor John Glover donated the land on the condition that it remain a city park. Subsequently, the new courthouse was built on the east side of the square, and the square was renamed Glover Park. During the Civil War, the square was used for training. Early photographs of the square show wagons assembled and stacked with cotton waiting to be brought to the market for processing. Old postcard images from the early twentieth century depict a tree-lined square with radiating walkways and a central cast-iron three-tiered fountain. The square was refurbished in the 1980s and still retains the walkways and fountain.

I was returning from a project interview in Roswell, Georgia, during the snowstorm of February 10, 2010. The roads were actually relatively empty, so I took advantage of my front-wheel drive Toyota and headed for the square. I tried to capture that moment just before sunset as the snow covered the shrubs, the sides of the tree trunks and the roof of the historic gazebo.

Marietta National Cemetery, Marietta, Cobb County

Located close to downtown Marietta, the National Cemetery is a beautiful, historic twenty-three-acre site that is easily seen behind a large surrounding stone wall. Originally established in 1866, the cemetery was intended to provide interment for nearly 10,000 Union dead from the Atlanta Campaign of the Civil War. The cemetery was originally known as the Marietta and Atlanta National Cemetery. It was placed in the National Register of Historic Places in 1998. As of 2006, there were 18,742 interments. It is currently closed to new burials. Marietta National Cemetery was laid out by Union army chaplain Thomas B. van Horne, who also laid out the Chattanooga National Cemetery. The northwest corner of the cemetery is anchored by this spectacular masonry archway. Originally designed by Montgomery C. Meigs, it is one of five similar masonry archways all designed by Meigs. The others are located at Arlington National Cemetery (1879), Chattanooga National Cemetery (1880), Vicksburg National Cemetery (1880) and Nashville National Cemetery (1870). Meigs was born in Augusta, Georgia, attended West Point, spent most of his military service with the Corps of Engineers, achieved the rank of brigadier general and served as quartermaster general of the army.

I first saw this magnificent masonry archway on a winter day in 2010. Snow had fallen, and I was driving around downtown Marietta looking for unique photo opportunities when I stumbled across the gateway. It

MARIETTA NATIONAL MILITARY CEMETERY
MARIETTA, GA.

is located a few blocks from the Marietta town square. I returned in the spring to do this sketch. I contacted the Veteran's Administration historian to learn about the unique architectural history of the gateway. The inscription above the arch reads, "Here rest the remains of 10,312 Officers and Soldiers who died in defense of the Union 1861–1865."

Brumby Hall, Marietta, Cobb County

The first superintendent of the Georgia Military Institute was Colonel Arnoldus V. Brumby. He built this Greek Revival residence in 1851 on the grounds of the campus. The institute property was the home of Marietta Country Club for many years, until it moved in the 1990s. Today, it is the home to the Marietta City Club golf course, hotel and conference center.

BRUMBY HALL - MARIETTA

Colonel Brumby, a West Point graduate, was the director of the institute from 1851 to 1859. During the Civil War, Brumby commanded the Fourteenth Georgia Regiment. When Sherman's troops occupied Marietta in 1864, the house was used as a hospital. The institute's buildings were burned following the Battle of Atlanta and the commencement of Sherman's March to the Sea. It is supposed that Brumby Hall was not burned because Brumby and Sherman were classmates and friends at West Point.

After the war, Brumby sold the house to Ellan M. Bradley. During that ownership, the property became known as The Hedges. In 1926, Howell and Katherine Trezvant purchased the home and undertook a major renovation and restoration. Hubert Bond Owens, founder of the University of Georgia's School of Landscape Architecture, designed the formal gardens surrounding the home. The Trezvants' daughter, Tillie T. Moore Owenby, lived in the house for many years before selling it to the City of Marietta. Today, the house is the home of the city's Gone with the Wind Museum and is open for tours.

Metropolitan Atlanta

TEXACO SIGN, OLD DIXIE HIGHWAY, ACWORTH, COBB COUNTY

Texaco, or the Texas Company, was founded in 1901 as the Texas Fuel Company in Beaumont, Texas. It was founded after the discovery of the Spindletop oil field in January of that year. Spindletop was the first oil field found on the Gulf coast of the United States. Texaco is now an oil subsidiary of the Chevron Corporation.

This forgotten piece of roadside advertising sits behind a fence in a yard off Old Dixie Highway 9 (US 41) in Acworth. The logo began with a red star in a white circle as a reference to the "Lone Star" of Texas, but its corporate identity was magnified under the guidance of the well-known industrial designer Walter Dorwin Teague. Teague developed the sign design that became the brand icon for more than fifty years. The current logo uses a white star in a red circle. Texaco also played a major role in television with the *Texaco Star Theater* and the Texaco Presents television specials featuring Bob Hope. I can still hear the jingle, "You can trust your car to the man who wears the star." I loved the shape of the supporting column and the crooked little lights that were used to illuminate the sign.

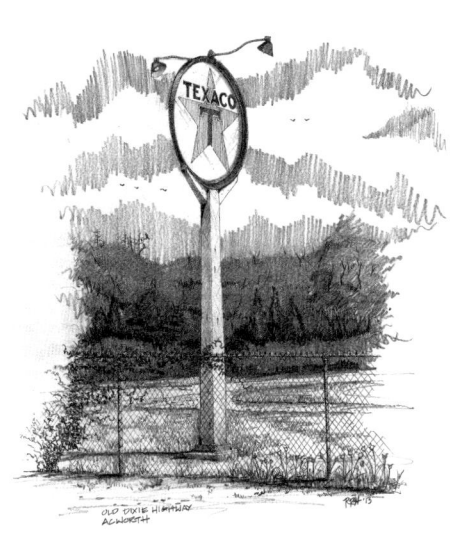

The City of Acworth has been a faithful client for nearly twenty-five years. I have worked with the city to revitalize the downtown commercial business district, which is bisected by the Old Dixie Highway. I had been working for the city for more than fifteen years before I spotted the sign, which is located north of the downtown district heading toward Bartow County.

A.J. White's Service Station, Old Dixie Highway, Cobb County

I have driven past this old gas station on Old Dixie Highway (US 41) dozens of times. I finally stopped in 2013 and decided to capture the look of the old place before it was gone. I do not know A.J. White, but the humble little gas station was probably his pride and joy during the 1950s and 1960s. The pumps were gone, the roof was starting to sag and a tree was growing out of the foundation, but I could still feel the hum of the now forgotten auto commerce. I loved the two-tone paint job that had almost crumbled off the side of the buildings. The old gas station was finally torn down in 2015, and the site remains vacant.

The Old Dixie Highway was an automobile highway or network of connected highways originally planned in 1914 to link the Midwest with the southeastern United States. Original plans were laid out by appointed state commissioners from Michigan, Illinois, Indiana, Ohio, Kentucky, Tennessee, North Carolina, South Carolina, Georgia and Florida. In Georgia, the Dixie Highway includes segments of US 41, US 278, US 441, Georgia State Route 24, US Route 31, US Route 301, Georgia State Route 21, US Route 17 and US Route 1. The Dixie Highway follows an

WHITE'S SERVICE STATION, ACWORTH

eastern route through coastal Georgia, including Augusta and Savannah, and a central route through Atlanta, Macon and Albany, with diagonal routes through Waycross and Milledgeville. The majority of US Highway 41 in Georgia, which extends from Chattanooga, Tennessee, through Atlanta, Macon and Albany, is considered part of Dixie Highway.

ROSENWALD SCHOOL, ACWORTH, COBB COUNTY

Construction began on the Acworth Rosenwald School in 1924. The Acworth African American community contributed $700 toward the cost of the school, and the Rosenwald Foundation matched that amount. An additional $1,850 was provided by the Cobb County Board of Education. Located on School Street, the building served as the only school for African Americans in Acworth from 1925 until 1948. Following the decision by the Cobb County Board of Education to construct a new school on School Street in 1949, the Rosenwald School was dismantled by members of the African American community and relocated to Cherokee Street. The building was reassembled and opened as a community center in 1953. The former school building has served as a community hall for the congregations of the nearby Bethel AME Church and the Zion Hill Baptist Church.

The son of Jewish immigrants, Julius Rosenwald began his career as a clothier in New York City. In 1895, his success brought him to the attention of Richard Sears, who needed a supplier for Sears, Roebuck & Company's mail-order business. Rosenwald provided the merchandise for men's suits. Rosenwald became a major shareholder and eventually a vice president for Sears. As sales grew dramatically under his leadership, Rosenwald was named president and board chairman in 1908. By 1912, Julius Rosenwald was one of the wealthiest men in Chicago, with a net worth over $23 million. A firm believer that wealth should be used to "cure the things that seem wrong," Rosenwald established the Rosenwald Fund to formalize the distribution of his wealth. Rosenwald supported Tuskegee Institute's Booker T. Washington's efforts to provide educational opportunities for African Americans and developed a plan to build schools for African American children. The Rosenwald School initiative eventually provided seed money for over 5,300 school-related buildings throughout the South.

The Well at Hyde Farm, Cobb County

Hyde Farm is an antebellum treasure in Cobb County. The main house and outbuildings represent a unique look back at the farmscape and agrarian lifestyle of the county before suburbanization. The farm was developed in the 1830s by the Power family and sold to the Hydes in the 1920s. The well has faithfully served the farm inhabitants for more than 150 years. There are eleven remaining structures from the early farm, including a log residence, chicken houses, barns, toolsheds, a goat house, an outhouse and the well.

Located along the Chattahoochee River, the farm was privately owned and operated as a farm from 1830 to 2004. The farm is located in one of the most affluent areas of metropolitan Atlanta. Encompassing more than ninety-five acres, the farm is located near Atlanta Country Club and is surrounded by large homes. Surprisingly, the Hyde family rejected multiple multimillion-dollar offers to buy the farm and remained living on the farm without indoor plumbing and electricity until the late 1980s. Following the passing of the Hydes, Cobb County, in association with the National Park Service and the Trust for Public Land, was able to negotiate

Metropolitan Atlanta

to purchase a portion of the farm. Forty acres of the farm, including all of the remaining buildings, are now owned by Cobb County. In 2013, my firm was selected by the county to prepare plans for the restoration of all of the extant farm buildings. Our work included preparation of measured drawings used to guide the restoration. The well is the first structure on the farm that I sketched. I was attracted to the use of the cedar logs and the hand-sawn lumber. The open structure allowed me to capture some of the landscape, including a fine old Osage orange tree in the background.

THE BARN AT HYDE FARM, COBB COUNTY

The barn at Hyde Farm is the centerpiece of a treasured antebellum farm that remained in production to the year 2004. The farm did not have running water or electricity until the late 1980s. The large barn is located on a high point overlooking a series of farm terraces that sits high above the Chattahoochee River. Built in the late 1800s, the barn was constructed with hand-sawn lumber harvested on site. The multicolored tin roof and the patched, twisted, knotted lumber really make it a unique piece of architecture.

THE BARN @ HYDE FARM

Other unique architectural buildings on the property include the original 1840s residence, a goat house, chicken houses, a hog shed, toolsheds, an outhouse, the well and a corn crib. The original residence has an existing stone fireplace and chimney built with stacked stone and clay mud. All of the extant buildings are supported with stacked stone foundation piers, and the main house was constructed with huge hand-hewn logs harvested on site.

Hyde Farm is a rare example of a twentieth-century historic vernacular farm. The site preserves one of the last remaining farms in Cobb County, with terraced fields, woodlands and historic structures dating to the nineteenth and early twentieth centuries. The Hyde Farm property was first settled by the Power family in the 1840s. The Powers ran a ferry crossing on the Chattahoochee River. Originally sharecroppers working for the Powers, the Hyde family purchased the farm in 1920. Soon after buying the farm, the Hydes began truck farming by selling eggs and sweet potatoes. The Hydes farmed the property until the death of J.C. Hyde in 2004. Today, the barn, the residence and the remaining outbuildings are restored and open to the public.

Metropolitan Atlanta

Kennesaw Mountain National Battlefield, Cobb County

Hundreds of thousands of Cobb County and Georgia residents climb the trail to the top of Kennesaw Mountain every year. The trail is popular year-round and takes about forty-five minutes to climb to reach the 1,800-foot summit. I raised my family in the shadow of the mountain and have enjoyed walking the trail for more than thirty years. I developed this sketch to give as a gift to a co-worker who was retiring. She told me that the trail was one of her favorite places in Georgia and hiking it was one of her favorite activities to do with her husband.

The Civil War Battle of Kennesaw Mountain took place in June 1864 and was one of the many battles that were part of General Sherman's Atlanta Campaign. The Union's Army of the Tennessee led by General McPherson and the Army of the Cumberland led by General Thomas attacked the Confederates led by General Joseph Johnston. Believing General Johnston's line was too thin, General Sherman decided to create a deception along the Confederate flanks and ordered an attack in the center. General Thomas was able to penetrate the center, but the overall attack failed. The Union army was able to gain strategic ground, which eventually led to General Johnston's retreat from the mountain in early July.

Kennesaw Mountain National Battlefield Park was established to commemorate the 1864 Atlanta Campaign. The visitor center and park headquarters provide introductory information about the park and the battle. Living history programs are offered during the summer months. The park trails may be the most popular trails in the Atlanta area, with trails up the mountain to the summit and throughout the more than 2,923-acre park.

Sweet Potato Barn, Mable House, Mableton, Cobb County

The Sweet Potato Barn is located on the grounds of the historic Mable House. The Mable House was the antebellum residence of Robert Mable (1803–1885). Robert Mable immigrated to the United States around 1820 and found his way to Cobb County around 1843 after living and working in Savannah and Hancock County. He married Pheriby Aycock from Hancock County in 1838. He originally purchased three hundred acres in Cobb County from Denson Melton in a land lottery but had grown the farm to more than six hundred acres by 1860. The two-story plantation plain residence on the property is the centerpiece of a well-preserved collection of buildings, including the sweet potato house, a blacksmith shop, smokehouse, corn crib and kitchen house.

During the Civil War, the house was used as a field hospital for Union troops as part of the Campaign for Atlanta. It has been documented that Walter Gresham's Union troops (Fourth Division, XVII Corps, of McPherson's Army of the Tennessee) withdrew to the Mable Plantation

SWEET POTATO BARN
MABLE HOUSE

and camped there after threatening the left rear of Confederate General Johnston's Smyrna line at the Chattahoochee River. Walter Q. Gresham became secretary of state in the cabinet of Grover Cleveland from 1893 to 1895.

In 1881, Robert Mable conveyed a section of his land to the railroad. The town that grew around the railroad was named Mableton. Robert Mable died in 1885 and is buried in the family cemetery on the property. The sweet potato house was used to store or "cure" sweet potatoes until it was time to take them to market. Curing converts some of the starches into sugars, improves flavor, toughens skins and prolongs storage life. The building was heated by a wood- and coal-burning stove under the floor raised off the ground. The upper windows in the ceiling were probably to vent and allow heated air to escape.

Baptist Student Union, Georgia State University, Atlanta, Fulton County

This unique building dates from around 1892. The building is significant for the unique Victorian architecture, but more importantly, it was the location of the first Coca-Cola Bottling Company. Other uses for the building included a produce market, a ladies' lingerie shop, a plumbing shop, an arts and crafts shop and Brown's T.V. Repair Service for thirteen years. During World War II, it gained the reputation as being a house of ill repute. The upstairs was used as a boardinghouse for many years. In May 1969, the house was turned over to Georgia State College, now Georgia State University, for the members of the Baptist Student Union.

Georgia State University was founded in 1913 as a night school for the Georgia School of Technology (Georgia Tech). In the 1930s, it became the Atlanta Extension Center, and in 1947 it was renamed the Atlanta Division of the University of Georgia. In 1955, it became an autonomous school and was renamed the Georgia State College of Business Administration. With the addition of new academic programs, it became Georgia State College and eventually Georgia State University by 1969. Today, Georgia

State University is the largest institution of higher education in Georgia by enrollment with a student population around fifty-three thousand.

I ran across this building while working on a wall mural as part of enhancements to the nearby Auburn Avenue Cultural District. Located only one block from the Student Union, Auburn Avenue is well known as the commercial center for African Americans in Atlanta. The Martin Luther King home and King Center are also located nearby.

THE SWAN HOUSE, ATLANTA, FULTON COUNTY

The Swan House was built in 1926 as the home for the Edward H. Inman family. The Swan House gets its name from the extensive use of swan and bird motifs used throughout the interior and exterior of the three-story house. The house was designed by Philip Trammel Shutze of the Atlanta firm Hentz, Reid and Adler. Shutze was well known as one of the country's greatest neoclassical architects. Shutze studied in Europe under the coveted Rome Prize after graduating from Georgia Tech. The Swan House is considered one of his finest works. Originally set on twenty-eight acres, Shutze's design is notable for the strong connection between the house and the landscape. The gardens were inspired by the famous Palazzo Corsini in Rome. The sketch is of the back or western façade of the house that faces Andrews Drive in Buckhead. The house was purchased by the Atlanta Historical Society in 1966 and opened to the public in 1967. The house and grounds are now part of the Atlanta History Center Campus.

Philip T. Shutze (1890–1981) was a member of Georgia Tech's first graduating class in architecture. He was also a graduate of Columbia University in architecture. He attended the American Academy in Rome and became a fellow in the American Institute of Architects. Other well-known works in the Atlanta area designed by Shutze include the clubhouse at Eastlake Golf Club, the Academy of Medicine Building in Midtown Atlanta and the Citizen's and Southern Bank Building near Five Points in downtown Atlanta.

TECH TOWER, GEORGIA INSTITUTE OF TECHNOLOGY, ATLANTA, FULTON COUNTY

The Georgia Institute of Technology, commonly referred to as Georgia Tech, was founded in 1885 as part of plans to build an industrial economy after the Civil War. Today, Georgia Tech is considered one of the top public research universities in the country, organized around six colleges with an enrollment approaching thirty-three thousand students.

Tech Tower is the centerpiece of the campus. The iconic structure remains a strong symbol of the university and is still easily seen through the growing Atlanta skyline. The Victorian brick building was built in 1888 to house classrooms and is the oldest structure on campus. The building was designed by the Atlanta firm of Bruce and Morgan. The tower is seven stories tall and includes the iconic "TECH" letters, which were originally added in 1918 by the class of 1922. The building is no longer used for classes but still houses administrative offices. My son, Russell, attended Georgia Tech and graduated with a master's degree in digital media in 2016.

I originally sketched the Tower and sold prints as part of a fundraiser for a family in need during the Christmas holidays. The program was so successful that I have turned it into an annual employee fundraiser during the holidays, offering a wider variety of sketches to company employees for purchase and donation.

Bobby Jones Golf Course, Atlanta, Fulton County

Robert Tyre "Bobby" Jones Jr. was born in Atlanta in 1902. His home course was East Lake Golf Club, which currently hosts the Tour Championship. Bobby Jones won his first tournament in 1916 at the inaugural Georgia Amateur Championship. Bobby Jones qualified for his first U.S. Open at the age of eighteen in 1920. He won his first U.S. Open in 1923. Between 1923 and 1930, he won thirteen major championships. Jones is the only player to ever have won the Grand Slam in the same calendar year. In 1930, he won the British Amateur Championship, the British Open, the U.S. Open and the U.S. Amateur.

Outside of golf, Jones earned a bachelor's degree in mechanical engineering from Georgia Tech (1922), a bachelor's degree in English literature from Harvard University (1924) and in 1926 studied law at Emory University. When Jones retired from golf, he joined his father's law firm—Jones, Evans, Moore and Howell (now Alston & Bird)—in Atlanta. Jones is credited with the co-design of Augusta National Golf Course with Alister Mackenzie (1931–33).

I was walking a trail adjacent to the Bobby Jones Golf Course in Atlanta when I spotted this tree. It was breathtaking in its height and spread. I doodled in a golf cart just to capture the magnificent sense of scale. The golf course is located in the heart of a former Civil War battlefield that played host to the Battle for Peachtree Creek. I have always tried to keep an eye out for specimen trees. I suspect that this tremendous tree may have been around since the Civil War. The golf course opened in 1932 as the first public golf course in Atlanta and is named after the great amateur golfer and Atlanta native.

The Wren's Nest, Home of Joel Chandler Harris, Atlanta, Fulton County

The Wren's Nest is located just a mile or so from downtown Atlanta in an area referred to as the West End. At the time the house was built, around 1868, the West End was an unincorporated village connected to Atlanta by horse-drawn trolley. The original name of the house was Snapbean Farm, which is a strong reference to the area's rural atmosphere. Joel Chandler Harris purchased the home in 1881 and made substantial Victorian modifications such as the wrap-around porch. Harris hired the architect George Humphries to convert the original farmhouse into a magnificent Queen Anne Victorian in the Eastlake style. Eastlake architectural style is credited to the architect and writer Charles Eastlake. Typical components of the Eastlake style include geometric ornaments, spindles, low relief carvings and incised lines, asymmetrical façade, dominant front gables, overhanging eaves, shaped and Dutch gables, a covered front porch, monumental chimneys, leaded windows and painted balustrades. The house got its name after a wren built a nest and produced a family in the mailbox.

   Joel Chandler Harris is the author of the Uncle Remus stories originally published in 1881. *Uncle Remus: His Songs and Stories* is a collection of animal stories, songs and oral folklore collected from southern Black Americans. The stories are written in a dialect devised by Harris to represent a Deep South dialect. He was also an editor for the *Atlanta Constitution* newspaper. The house was designated a National Historic Landmark in 1962 and added to the National Register of Historic Places in 1966. I first saw the Wren's Nest when my firm was asked to prepare plans to improve the sidewalks in the block that included the house.

A Scenic Georgia Sketchbook

Big Bethel AME Church, Auburn Avenue, Atlanta, Fulton County

Big Bethel AME Church was founded in 1847 and is the oldest predominantly African American congregation in the Metropolitan Atlanta area. Historical records indicate that the church was formed prior to the incorporation of Atlanta on December 28, 1847. It was established as the first Black church in Marthasville (Atlanta), and it was Methodist. After the Civil War, the congregation associated with the AME Church, which became the first independent denomination in the country. Big Bethel became the center of the community and a focal point for social action. The first public school for African Americans was founded in the basement of the church in 1879. In 1881, Morris Brown College, the

BETHEL AME CHURCH, AUBURN AVE, ATLANTA

only college in Georgia started solely by African Americans, held classes in the basement of Big Bethel before moving to its first campus.

Big Bethel was known as "Sweet Auburn's City Hall" after the famous African American commercial district located along Auburn Avenue in Atlanta. In 1911, President William H. Taft spoke from the pulpit, and in 1990 Nelson Mandela spoke there.

The existing building was built in 1891 and rebuilt in 1922 after being destroyed by fire in 1920. In 1922, the new building was erected with the lighted cross in the steeple with the message "Jesus Saves." All of the walls, except the west wall, are original (before the fire). AME (African Methodist Episcopal) Churches grew out of the Free African Society (FAS), established in Philadelphia in 1787. The church steeple is an icon of the Atlanta skyline and highly visible from the elevated section of Interstate 75/85 that passes close by the church.

FIVE POINTS, ATLANTA, FULTON COUNTY

An enormous Coca-Cola sign sits on top of the Olympia Building in downtown Atlanta at Five Points. The building was erected between 1935 and 1936 by Frank Hawkins, the founder of the Third National Bank, but it was not the original location for the sign. The Coca-Cola sign has been standing on top of the building only since 2003. The retro-style sign structure is thirty-three feet in diameter and features nine-foot-tall, twenty-nine-feet-wide Coca-Cola lettering. The original location for the neon sign was in the front of the Candler building (Margaret Mitchell Square), where it stood from 1932 to 1981. The Candler building is located several blocks north of Five Points.

Five Points in downtown Atlanta is the intersection of Peachtree Street (including the renamed section of Whitehall Street), Marietta Street, Edgewood Avenue and Decatur

Street. Generally, the five-point intersection, or "Five Points" as it is known to Atlantans, represents the center of the city. Five Points was originally the intersection of two Creek Indian trails: the "Pitch Tree" Trail (evolved into Peachtree) and the Sandtown Trail. In 1845, a grocery store was opened adjacent to Five Points and later served as the city's first post office. In 1875, Atlanta's drinking water system began with the construction of three artesian wells at Five Points. The center of the city has shifted north from Five Points, and the commercial and business hubs of the city have spread to include major centers in the northern suburbs and Buckhead. Five Points remains a hub of activity, as the campus of Georgia State University has grown to encompass many of the buildings around Five Points. Georgia State University is the state's largest public university with a student body approaching fifty-five thousand.

Oakland Cemetery, Atlanta, Fulton County

Oakland Cemetery was established in 1850. The eighty-eight-acre cemetery is notable for the interments of Margaret Mitchell (author of *Gone with the Wind*), Bobby Jones (the golfer and grand slam champion), Maynard Jackson (Atlanta's first African American mayor) and many other local and state politicians. There is also a large section of Civil War burials (an estimated 6,900), including five Confederate generals and a section for formerly enslaved people. Shortly after the Civil War ended, a few thousand fallen soldiers from the Atlanta Campaign who were previously buried in battleground graves were moved to Oakland Cemetery. The Confederate section is marked by a sixty-five-foot obelisk, which was the tallest structure in Atlanta for many years.

The cemetery was designed as part of the "rural" cemetery movement and is beautifully landscaped. The entry gate was built in 1896 and designed by Bruce & Morgan Architects (the same firm that designed the Georgia Tech Administration building). Porter King was the mayor of Atlanta at that time.

An estimated seventy thousand people are interred at Oakland Cemetery. The last plots were sold in 1884. Additional notable burials include twenty-seven former Atlanta mayors, six Georgia governors and architect André Steiner (1908–2009). Steiner was a Holocaust survivor

Oakland Cemetery, Atlanta.

and the first director of my former firm's planning and urban design department (Robert and Company). He was a Bauhaus-educated architect who escaped Germany. He immigrated to Atlanta from Cuba in the 1950s. He was responsible for the original master plans for Jekyll Island, Stone Mountain Park and Callaway Gardens. I had the opportunity to meet André in the early 1990s, and he immediately impressed me with his energy. I took over as the third director following James Cothran in 1997. Cothran was also a well-known landscape architect and author; he died in 2012.

A Scenic Georgia Sketchbook

Gateway Monument, Buckhead, Atlanta, Fulton County

Buckhead is a commercial and residential district within Atlanta located a couple of miles from downtown. It is widely considered a separate business district as compared to downtown and midtown Atlanta. The commercial area is centered on the intersection of Peachtree Road, Paces Ferry Road and Piedmont Road. Buckhead is the home of Lenox Square. Built in 1959, it was one of the first malls in the country and the largest shopping center in the Southeast.

Metropolitan Atlanta

The name *Buckhead* comes from a story regarding a large deer that was killed and the head placed in a prominent location. By the late 1800s, Buckhead had become a spot for wealthy Atlantans, and development was dominated by country estates. Buckhead was annexed into Atlanta in 1952.

Today, Buckhead is one of the wealthiest zip codes in the nation. Buckhead is regularly ranked as one of the nation's most affluent communities. The Georgia Governor's Mansion is located on Paces Ferry Road in Buckhead as well as the Atlanta History Center.

The masonry gateway monument is located on Paces Ferry Road. The gateway stands alone along the edge of the roadway. I do not know the history of the gateway, but it symbolizes the "country estate" affluence of the historic Buckhead residential areas.

Bulloch Hall, Roswell, Fulton County

Bulloch Hall is a Greek Revival antebellum home built in 1839. It is the former home of Martha Bulloch Roosevelt, the mother of Teddy Roosevelt, the twenty-sixth president of the United States. President Roosevelt visited the house in 1905, and Eleanor Roosevelt visited many times. Margaret Mitchell, author of *Gone with the Wind*, also visited the house, and it may have been the inspiration for Tara. The home is listed in the National Register of Historic Places. Adjacent to the home is a beautiful kitchen garden that is entered through this wooden arbor with a built-in seat. I prepared a master plan for the property in the late 1990s.

Bulloch Hall is one of several historically significant buildings in Roswell, including Barrington Hall, Smith Plantation and the Roswell Mills. All of these properties are antebellum. In July 1864, the Union army began an eleven-day occupation of the city. During this time, the mills were still operating. The Union army destroyed the mills, and approximately four hundred workers (mostly women) were deported north to work in northern factories. Most of the four hundred never returned to the South. The mills were supplying cloth and yarn to the Confederate government from 1861 to 1864. Barrington Hall is another Greek Revival mansion built as the residence of Barrington King. Barrington King and his father founded the town of Roswell and developed the mills.

Bulloch Hall, Barrington Hall and the Smith Plantation are operated as house museums. Barrington Hall also includes one of the only surviving antebellum gardens.

Agnes Scott College, McCain Entrance, Decatur, DeKalb County

Agnes Scott College was founded in 1889 as a Presbyterian female seminary. The name was changed to Agnes Scott Institute in 1890 in honor of the mother of the school's primary benefactor, Colonel George Washington Scott. The institution became Agnes Scott College in 1906. The entire campus is listed in the National Register of Historic Places and located within walking distance of downtown Decatur. The "McCain" entrance was built in 1950 and is the primary pedestrian connection to downtown Decatur. James Ross McCain served as the second president of the college from 1923 to 1951. The McCain entrance presides over a walkway leading to Agnes Scott Hall or "Old Main" as it is now known. Agnes Scott Hall is a three-story brick building housing a dormitory and administrative office. Originally designed by the locally prominent architecture firm of Bruce and Morgan, it was built in 1891. Thomas H. Morgan was one of the founders of the American Institute of Architects in Georgia and the first registered architect in Georgia, with registration

Entry gate @ Agnes Scott College, Decatur

number one. He also designed buildings at Georgia Tech (15 Tech Tower) and Oglethorpe University.

My great-aunt Nell Esslinger attended Agnes Scott College and graduated in 1923. She moved to New York City with my grandfather in 1923 and became a professional musician and opera singer before settling into a career as a music teacher. In all probability, she lived in Old Main while she was attending Agnes Scott College.

Agnes Scott College is a private women's liberal arts college with an enrollment of approximately one thousand students. It is located just a few miles east of Atlanta. Agnes Scott College is one of only 92 all-women colleges in the country. (In 1960, there were 259.)

Main Gate at Emory University, Decatur, DeKalb County

Emory University is the second-oldest private university in Georgia. Emory University has the sixteenth-largest endowment among U.S.

colleges and universities, including substantial gifts in Coca-Cola stock. Emory University has established a strong reputation for education in law, medicine, theology, business and liberal arts. The campus features buildings designed by well-known architects, including Paul Rudolph (the Cannon Chapel), Michael Graves (Michael C. Carlos Museum) and John Portman (Coca-Cola Commons and the Dobbs University Center). Current enrollment includes around fifteen thousand students.

I was attending an orchestra concert at Emory University and stopped to sketch the main gate to the campus. The marble and wrought-iron gate is beautifully landscaped and presents a stunning public display. Founded in 1836, Emory moved to Decatur (a few miles east of Atlanta) and was chartered as a university in 1915. The Haygood-Hopkins Memorial Gateway marks the main entrance to the campus. The left pillar is dedicated to Atticus Greene Haygood, and the right pillar is dedicated to Isaac Stiles Hopkins, former presidents of the university. The gateway was gifted to the university in 1937 by Linton B. Robeson, class of 1886.

Metropolitan Atlanta

OLD CAMPBELL COUNTY COURTHOUSE, FAIRBURN, FULTON COUNTY

Campbell County was a Georgia county from 1828 to 1931. Portions of the county north of the Chattahoochee River became part of Douglas County in 1870 and the remainder south of the river became part of Fulton County in 1931. The original Campbell County Courthouse was located near the intersection of Cascade Palmetto Highway and Campbellton-Fairburn Road in what is now the city of Chattahoochee Hills. The original courthouse is gone but is commemorated with a stone marker. The second

OLD CAMPBELL COUNTY COURTHOUSE

courthouse sits one block from the railroad in downtown Fairburn, which was the county seat of Campbell County back in 1870. The Greek Revival Campbell County Courthouse was built in 1871 (only six years after the Civil War) and is listed in the National Register of Historic Places.

The courthouse was built with brick molded locally. The brick walls are sixteen inches thick. The courthouse was built by a local Palmetto contractor, Smith and Brother, for $10,674. Remodeling in 1907 added plumbing, heating and light fixtures. The enormous portico columns are twenty feet tall and three feet in diameter. They are molded from concrete. No exterior alterations have been made to the courthouse since its original construction. Offices were located on the first floor, and the main courtroom was on the second floor. For thirty years between 1940 and 1970, the courthouse housed a branch of the Atlanta Public Library and a recreation center.

I prepared this sketch to help illustrate a downtown master plan my firm was preparing in the late 1980s for Fairburn. Today, the courthouse still stands and is used as the home for the local Campbell County Historical Society. The original sketch was drawn on yellow trace paper.

Dillard's Hardware Store, Fairburn, Fulton County

I was working on the master plan for the Fairburn historic downtown commercial district in the late 1980s when I spotted this old hardware store. The character of the building, the sidewalk displays and the old window lettering caught my attention. Today, the store and the building are gone, and the city built a small pocket park and amphitheater on the vacant lot.

Fairburn is approximately ten to fifteen miles southwest of Atlanta and was incorporated in 1854. Located along the former Atlanta & West Point Railroad, the city was affected by the Civil War. Much of the railroad was destroyed by Sherman's forces in August 1864. The Federal army spent two days in Fairburn burning railroad ties, bending rails and looting and pillaging local residents. On August 29, Sherman ordered his troops to march toward Jonesboro, which is located twenty miles southeast of Fairburn. Fairburn became the county seat of Campbell County, which was established in 1871. Campbell County went bankrupt during the Great Depression and was absorbed into Fulton County in 1932.

Metropolitan Atlanta

Dillard's Hardware, Fairburn

Descendants of the Dillards discovered this sketch on my website and reached out to me to briefly share stories of growing up as children in Fairburn and playing in their father's store. The original sketch was drawn on yellow trace paper.

Downtown Fairburn, Fulton County

Fairburn was incorporated in 1854. It is located along the CSX railroad line. Early records indicate that the city was settled as early as 1830 as the city of Cartersville. The name was changed one year later to Berryville. The name *Fairburn* is believed to come from a township in the County of York, England. The original state charter set the jurisdiction of the city in 1854 as all land within a six-hundred-yard radius of the railroad depot. By 1871, the city limits had expanded to a half-mile radius and included six dry goods stores, five groceries, a hotel, a printing press, a local newspaper, four saloons, factories, two marble yards, several cotton gins and an oil mill. Sanborn Fire Insurance maps from 1892 and 1921 offer a glimpse of the city and show a mixture of brick and frame buildings along Main Street (also called Depot

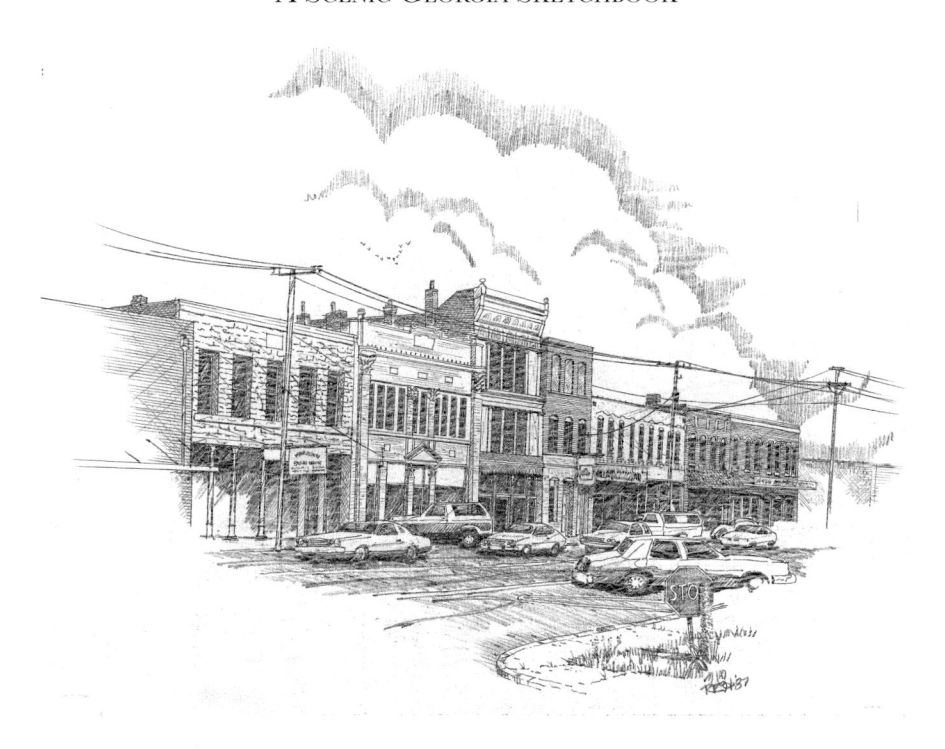

Street). Across the street from commercial Main Street were a passenger depot and one for freight, both of which are still there today. The downtown commercial district of Fairburn, including twenty downtown buildings and the two train depots, is listed in the National Register of Historic Places.

You can tell from the old automobiles that I made this sketch in the late 1980s. I was working on a master plan for the historic downtown commercial district. I loved the chevron shape to the Main Street and the rising old cast-iron building in the center. The street scene has not changed, with the exception that the third building from the right (old Dillard's Hardware Store) is gone. The original sketch was drawn on yellow trace paper.

Quarters 10, Fort McPherson, Atlanta, Fulton County

Quarters 10 is located adjacent to the parade ground in the central historic district on what was Fort McPherson in Atlanta. My firm was selected to prepare an illustrated design guideline for the military base before it was

Metropolitan Atlanta

closed. While I was photographing this building, the commanding general's wife and resident of this spectacular home stopped me and asked if I wanted a tour of the inside. It was an incredible opportunity that I could not decline. She told me that the ten-thousand-square-foot home had been used by Dwight Eisenhower, and he had added the upper-level screened-in back porch for sleeping. I prepared the sketch and gave it to the general's wife as a thank-you for her gracious hospitality.

Fort McPherson was established as a military post by authority of the Sundry Civil Bill approved by Congress on March 3, 1885. The bill included $15,000 to purchase land and construct a ten-company post. By the summer of 1889, most of the installation's historic district was constructed for a total of only $400,000. It is named in honor of Union major general James Birdseye McPherson, U.S. Volunteers. He was killed on July 22, 1864, during the Battle of Atlanta. During World War I, Fort McPherson housed prisoners from the Imperial German navy.

The Fort McPherson Historic District was designated in 1975. The boundaries of the district encompass forty-one buildings. Visually, the buildings within the district are bound together by the formal layout around the parade field and the High Victorian architectural style. Fort McPherson is located approximately two and a half miles south of downtown Atlanta. Today, Fort McPherson is closed. Portions of the installation are being used for movie studios, and the remainder is being redeveloped as a mixed-use community.

Guardhouse, Fort McPherson, Atlanta, Fulton County

The site selected for the new ten-company post was located two and a half miles south of the original McPherson Barracks, which was deactivated in October 1881. Today, the site of the original McPherson Barracks is occupied by Spelman College. The site for the new Fort McPherson was purchased for $15,000 and totaled only 140 acres. Before construction began on the new installation, an additional 96 acres was purchased along the Central of Georgia Railway for $14,740. By August 1886 the original boundaries for the 236-acre post had been established.

Under the command of the quartermaster general, Captain Joshua West Jacobs, assistant quartermaster, was assigned the job of supervising the construction of the new post. The new post, as designed by Captain Jacobs, consisted of officers' quarters, barracks, a post headquarters, a hospital, a bakery, a guardhouse and stables. By the summer of 1889, most of the installation's historic district had been constructed for a grand total of only $400,000. The installation was named for Major General James Birdseye McPherson, U.S. Volunteers, who fought alongside General Sherman in the Atlanta Campaign of the Civil War.

The guardhouse, originally identified as Building 51, is positioned between the historic parade field and the original entrance at Lee Street (US 29). When I sketched the building in 1988, the building was used as the post telephone exchange. At that time, Fort McPherson was the home of U.S. Army Forces Command (FORSCOM) and the Third U.S. Army Headquarters. Fort McPherson had approximately 4,300 military personnel and 5,250 civilian employees.

Confederate Monument, Douglasville, Douglas County

There are an estimated 175 Confederate monuments and public memorials remaining in Georgia. Stone Mountain Park, owned by the State of Georgia, is designated as a "Memorial to the Confederacy" and is by far the largest in the state. Stone Mountain Park includes a carving of President Jefferson Davis and Generals Robert E. Lee and Thomas J. Stonewall Jackson. The carving on the mountain measures 76 feet by 158 feet and is 400 feet above the ground. The majority of the remaining monuments can be found on courthouse lawns and public squares all across the state. Typically, the memorials take the form of an obelisk with a Confederate soldier or Confederate flag. According to tradition, the Confederate soldier is always oriented facing north. The uniformed Confederate soldier stands on picket duty, holding his musket by the barrel on his proper right side, the butt rests by his right foot. Many of these monuments were funded and placed by the United Daughters of the Confederacy.

I sketched this monument, located on the former Douglas County Courthouse grounds, in 1988 while working on a project in downtown Douglasville. I was struck by this simple but powerful symbol of Confederate pride that is seen on courthouse lawns all across Georgia juxtaposed against the modern 1950s courthouse. Today, the modernist courthouse has been converted into a museum for local and regional history. The Confederate monument has been relocated to the lawn at the new courthouse, built in 1998. The monument commemorates Confederate soldiers of Douglas County and was erected by the Douglasville chapter of the United Daughters of the Confederacy.

Metropolitan Atlanta

Starr's Mill, Fayette County

There are dozens of roads around metro Atlanta that are named after historic mills, such as Howell Mill Road, Moore's Mill Road and Brown's Mill Road. The original location for many of the mills can be found documented on maps from the Civil War. The majority of those mills date back to the 1820s and 1830s. They were typically built along streams that could be channeled and directed for waterpower. The mills were used to grind flour and corn (gristmills), provide power for sewing and weaving (woolen mills), cut lumber (lumber mills and sawmills), grind sugar cane (syrup mills) and gin cotton (cotton mill).

I was returning from a client meeting with the City of Senoia when I stumbled across Starr's Mill on my way back to Atlanta. I was immediately struck by the scenic beauty of the old mill and spillway sitting on Whitewater Creek. Based on the Georgia Historic Marker on site, there has been a mill in this location since the mid-1820s. The mill was named after Hilliard Starr, who purchased and operated the mill after the Civil War. The current structure dates from 1907 and operated as a mill until 1959. The mill and the surrounding land and pond are now part of a Fayette County Park.

Administration Building, Fort Gillem, Clayton County

Fort Gillem is located south of Atlanta in Forest Park, Clayton County. It was built by the U.S. Army in 1940 as a satellite installation to nearby Fort McPherson. The base was used for supply and included the Atlanta Quartermaster Depot and the Atlanta Ordnance Depot. The consolidated installation became known operationally as the Atlanta Army Depot. The Atlanta Army Depot was deactivated in 1974. In 2005, the Base Realignment and Closure Commission recommended that Fort Gillem be closed. The majority of the base was purchased by the City of Forest Park in 2012. Due to environmental contamination issues and a slow recovery from the recession, the base property has been slow to redevelop. The fort was named in the memory of Lieutenant General Alvan Cullom Gillem Jr.

My firm was selected to develop a design manual for Fort Gillem in the late 1980s. The landscape at Fort Gillem was dominated by warehouses and railroad sidings. Located at one end of the base was the housing and administration complex. At the time that I sketched the administration building, it was the headquarters for the First Army Garrison. Fort Gillem is located east of Hartsfield Jackson International Airport. It used to be very easy to spot Fort Gillem during approaches to the airport. The massive warehouse roofs and railroad complex were unique and easy to spot from an airplane window. Fort Gillem was closed in 2011.

Wick's Tavern, Villa Rica, Carroll County

Gold was discovered in the vicinity of Villa Rica in 1826. At that time, there was a pair of small communities: Hixtown and Cheevetown. Named for William Hix and Allison Cheeves, the two towns located one mile apart combined to become the city of Villa Rica, incorporated in 1881. Villa Rica stands for "rich village."

Wick's Tavern was originally built in the city of Hixtown but was moved to its current location one block behind Main Street in downtown Villa Rica in 1998. The tavern was built in 1830 and is considered the oldest commercial structure in Carroll County. It was built by John B. Wick and

Wick's Tavern, Villa Rica.

was a gathering place for gold miners in the early nineteenth century. At the peak of the gold rush, there were nineteen commercial gold operations around Villa Rica.

Architecturally, Wick's Tavern is unique and represents the "Dutch" style of timber framing. Dutch-style framing refers to the high posts along the eave walls and the tie beam (or anchor beams) that connects into the posts near a top plate with wedged dovetailed through tenons. By placing posts close together, there is no need for central posts or floor joists on the second floor. Currently, Wick's Tavern is vacant and in need of repair and restoration.

Villa Rica is also the birthplace of Thomas Dorsey, known as the "father of Black gospel music." He was born in 1899, and his best-known composition is "Take My Hand, Precious Lord," which was a favorite song of Martin Luther King Jr.

Tenant House at McDaniel Farm Park, Duluth, Gwinnett County

The original land that became the McDaniel farm was sold in the land lottery in 1820. The 134-acre tract was purchased by the McDaniel family on the courthouse steps as part of an estate auction in 1859. They paid $450 for the farm. The McDaniel family farmed the property continuously from 1859 until 1999—most of that time without electricity or the benefit of motorized tractors. Archie McDaniel, the great-grandson of the founder, took control of the farm at the ripe old age of twelve in 1933 following the passing of his father, John. Archie and his wife, Louise, lived on the farm until Archie's passing in 1999. The original house, built in 1874, has been restored along with many of the farm's original buildings, including a barn, carriage house, well house, chicken coop, buggy shed, blacksmith shed and tenant house. The farm is called a "subsistence" farm, meaning it produced everything needed to live, including the lumber to build the house and outbuildings.

Tenant houses or sharecroppers' houses are a common sight along many rural roads all over Georgia. Tenant farmers were a key component of the farm economy before mechanization. The farm's landowner would allow the tenant to use the land in return for a share of the crops produced. In many cases, the tenant farmers owned their own equipment and mules. Sharecroppers were generally poorer and did not own anything.

TENANT HOUSE @ MCDANIEL FARM

Sharecropping was used extensively in the South during Reconstruction. Following the Civil War, southern planters were land rich but had very little money. Formerly enslaved people could provide labor but had no money or land. As a result, a sharecropping system was developed with a focus on harvesting cotton or tobacco to provide income for the landowner and the sharecropper. Poor white farmers also became sharecroppers, as famously described in Erskine Caldwell's novel *Tobacco Road*. Based on a McDaniel family ledger, they paid their tenant farm laborers ten cents per hour and traded food and household items for wages. Planting and picking cotton was the primary task of their tenant farmers. Tenant farming had just about disappeared by the beginning of World War II due to the use of motorized tractors and the decline in the cotton industry.

THE ROOT HOUSE, MARIETTA, COBB COUNTY

The Root House was built in 1845 for Hannah and William Root. William Root was Marietta's first druggist. He was born in Philadelphia and moved to Marietta in 1839 to open a drug/mercantile store. The home was originally located on the corner of Church and Lemon Streets. The

Roots owned the home from 1845 until 1886. In 1893, the house was moved to another location on Lemon Street and underwent a Victorian remodeling that was popular at that time. The Root house remained a single-family residence until the 1940s. At that time, the home was subdivided into apartments and eventually fell into disrepair. In 1989, the Cobb Landmarks and Historical Society acquired the house and moved it to its current location on the corner of Polk Street and the North Marietta Parkway. The exterior has been restored to 1845, and the interior has been furnished with period antiques from the 1860s.

The Root House is architecturally referred to as having a "Plantation Plain" style, otherwise known as an I-house. I have run across Plantation Plain homes all over Georgia. The style is typically similar to hall and parlor houses that are only two rooms wide and one room deep with a central hallway. The Plantation Plain house or I-house will have a second story that rises above and may or may not include windows in the second story. There are usually chimneys on both ends of the house, and kitchens were often added perpendicular to the rear of the house. A full or partial front porch is also very common. I first encountered this building form during preparation of an analysis of the historic resources in the Central Savannah Region of Georgia, including roughly the thirteen counties surrounding Augusta along the Savannah River. Antebellum southern homes were more typically of this style than the romanticized versions associated with *Gone with the Wind*. I developed a master plan for the Root House site in the early 2000s to support efforts to expand the property and protect it from commercial encroachment. Today, the site includes a freestanding kitchen house, slave cabin and visitor's center.

2

SOUTH GEORGIA

*Making my own mark on a blank sheet feels the best
and where I can be myself the most.*
—*Joel Russell Huffman*

In the past thirty years, I have had the wonderful opportunity to work across South Georgia, including work in Albany and Dougherty County, Leesburg and Lee County, Tifton and Tift County, Waycross and Ware County, Camden County and St. Mary's, Brunswick and Glynn County and Savannah and Chatham County. I have found the landscape of South Georgia to be highly varied and at times breathtaking. In addition to the endless acres of pine forest, there are unique treasures such as the lime sinks in the Southwest, the great Okefenokee Swamp in the southeast and the magnificent historic districts in Savannah. Every time I see a cotton field ready for harvest looking like a blanket of snow across the landscape, it takes my breath away. I have also long admired the unusual, ethereal beauty of a pecan orchard with the rows and rows of canopy trees that seem to go on for miles.

Beginning in the early 1990s, I began working in Waycross and Ware County. One of my projects was the design of a bike trail to the north entrance of the Okefenokee Swamp. The cypress swamp is full of mystery and natural wonder rivaled only by the everglades in Florida. In the mid-1990s, I began working in Albany and Dougherty County planning for the reuse of Radium Springs following the floods in 1994 and 1998. Radium

Springs is one of the seven Natural Wonders in Georgia. The bubbling blue hole spring has clean, cool waters that glow in a brilliant aqua blue that contributed to its name. In the 1990s, I also began working with the City of Savannah on the design and planning for the renovation of some of their wonderful parks. General Oglethorpe's plan for Savannah created a legacy of park "squares" that is the key to the beauty of the city's historic district. Jekyll Island is by far one of my favorite destinations in Georgia. The former playground for the wealthy robber barons of the late nineteenth century is a treasure of historic buildings and landscapes.

Project Notes

I have worked for many years in South Georgia on some unique and wonderful projects. I began working in Savannah with the master planning for upgrades to historic Daffin Park. Daffin Park was originally designed by landscape architect John Nolen in 1906–7. Daffin Park was the first park in the city to be designed by a professional. I also spent some time on nearby Tybee Island after my firm was selected to do a parking study for the entire island. Tybee is located a few miles outside of Savannah and used to be called Savannah Beach. The parking study resulted in the design for the streetscape enhancements and roundabout along South Beach Street. In the early 1990s, my firm was selected to prepare a master plan for the City of Waycross, which eventually led to the opportunity to redesign historic Plant Park as part of a federal grant program. In the late 1990s, my firm was selected to design a master plan for the parks in Albany–Dougherty County.

My favorite projects in Albany–Dougherty County include multiple phases of work at historic Radium Springs, as well as renovations to Carver Park, Thorton Community Park and the Gordon Sports Complex.

Recent work in South Georgia includes multiple phases of streetscape enhancements in historic downtown Tifton. Other recent work in the region includes a Joint Land Use Study for the King's Bay Naval Submarine Base in Camden County and the design of a memorial sculpture to the victims of the lethal tornadoes that struck Dougherty County in 2017.

List of Illustrations

36. Forsyth Park Fountain, Savannah, Chatham County
37. The Lucas Theater, Savannah, Chatham County
38. Walls, Fences and Gates, Savannah, Chatham County
39. Tybee Island Lighthouse, Chatham County
40. Jekyll Island Gatehouse, Glynn County
41. Jekyll Island Club Hotel, Glynn County
42. Tabby Sugar Works, Camden County
43. Plant Park Fountain, Waycross, Ware County
44. Tift Theater, Tifton, Tift County
45. Fulwood Park, Tifton, Tift County
46. Radium Springs Gazebo, Albany, Dougherty County
47. Radium Springs Ticket Booth, Dougherty County
48. Gateway Arch, Dougherty County/Mitchell County

Forsyth Park Fountain, Savannah, Chatham County

Forsyth Park was originally called Hodgson Park and was only ten acres. William Brown Hodgson (1801–1871) conceived of the idea of setting aside ten acres of wooded land for development as Savannah's first recreational park. The park was expanded in 1867 to thirty acres and renamed Forsyth Park. The iconic fountain was placed in 1858. It has become a symbol for the city of Savannah. The fountain was manufactured by Jones, Beebe & Company, an ironworks foundry in the Bronx, New York. The cost in 1858 was $3,000. The inspiration for the design of the cast-iron fountain is believed to be the Great Exhibition held in London in 1851 at the Crystal Palace. Jones, Beebe & Company used the pattern exhibited at the Crystal Palace fountain as inspiration. That fountain was designed by Michael Joseph Napoleon Lienard. The company first offered the fountain in 1855.

The original fountain included four tritons that were replaced with urns. Swans were added for balance. There are at least three other cities with the same fountain, including Madison, Indiana; Poughkeepsie, New York; and Cuzco, Peru. The fountain in Madison, Indiana, was dedicated in 1886. It is purported to have been used at the Philadelphia Centennial Exposition

FORSYTH PARK - SAVANNAH

and was manufactured by James and Kirtland in New York. I have seen both fountains, and they are identical with the exception of the pool and surrounding accents. The Soldiers Memorial Fountain in Poughkeepsie, New York, was unveiled in 1870 to honor veterans of the Civil War. Its cost at the time was $4,000.

Forsyth Park was originally named for Georgia governor John Forsyth (1780–1841). William Bischoff created the original landscape design for the park. The south end (opposite from the fountain) was originally added as a military parade ground. Dummy forts built in 1909 were used for training during World War I and are still in the park as walled courtyard gardens.

South Georgia

THE LUCAS THEATER, SAVANNAH, CHATHAM COUNTY

The Lucas Theater was built by Arthur Melville Lucas Jr. in 1921 and has a seating capacity of 1,200. Arthur Lucas was a businessman who grew up in Savannah and had wide-ranging business interests, including newspapers, banks, a Ford dealership and a department store. He was also heavily invested in the motion picture business. He eventually became president of the American Theater Corporation in 1920 and led the construction of more than forty theaters across the South. The Lucas Theater in Savannah is the only theater bearing his name.

The architect for the theater was C.K. Howell, and construction began in 1920. The construction cost is estimated to have been around $500,000 at that time. The theater opened on December 26, 1921. The premiere on opening night included two films: *Hard Luck*, starring Buster Keaton, and *Camille*, starring Alla Nazimova and Rudolph Valentino. The Lucas Theater was the first building in Savannah with air conditioning when it was installed in 1926. The theater changed ownership through the years and was eventually threatened with demolition to make room for a parking lot. In 1987, a nonprofit was formed to save the theater, and restoration began in 1995. The grand reopening was held in December 2000, with three showings of *Gone with the Wind*. Today, the theater nonprofit has joined forces with the Savannah College of Art and Design and hosts a wide variety of programs. The theater sits adjacent to Reynolds Square on the corner with Congress and Abercorn Streets.

LUCAS THEATER, SAVANNAH

A Scenic Georgia Sketchbook

Walls, Fences and Gates, Savannah, Chatham County

Throughout the Historic District of Savannah is a cornucopia of fences and walls and unique architectural details that combine to create and contribute to the lasting imagery of the city. The sketches I included in this book represent a small sampling of what can be found within a short walk of any of the downtown hotels. I first visited Savannah on a college field trip in 1980 and quickly became enamored with the city's history and rich architectural heritage. I have visited Savannah at least twice a year for the past forty years and always find something new to sketch.

The city of Savannah was laid out by General James Edward Oglethorpe, a member of the British Parliament since 1722. In an effort to establish an English colony between South Carolina and Florida, as part of the "Georgia Movement" (named for King George), Oglethorpe and a group of colonists, estimated around one hundred and accompanied by Colonel William Bull, the royal governor of South Carolina and an experienced surveyor, landed at Savannah on February 12, 1733. Plans were put in place by Oglethorpe to build a town on a high bluff overlooking the Savannah River. The site selected was sixteen miles inland from the Atlantic Ocean at Yamacraw Bluff and was chosen based on approval received from Chief Tomochichi of the local Yamacraw Indians.

Oglethorpe and Bull laid out the new town of Savannah around a series of public squares, likely modeled after eighteenth-century London grid patterns. Today, the public squares are a signature element of the historic district that runs along the Savannah River. The public squares are all unique treasures unto themselves adorned with sculpture and memorials and typically shaded by magnificent live oak trees.

South Georgia

A Scenic Georgia Sketchbook

South Georgia

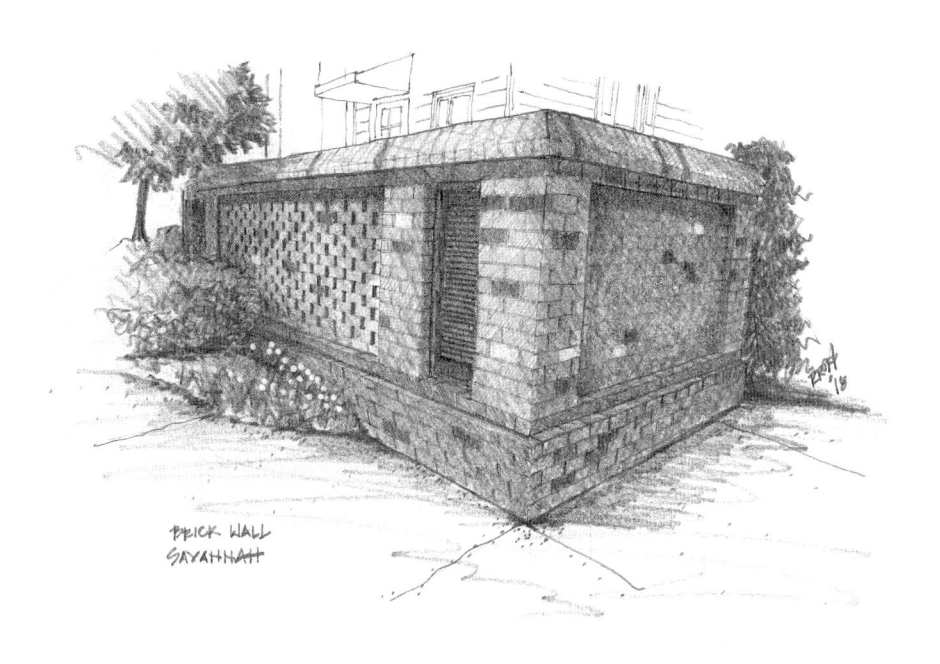

TYBEE ISLAND LIGHTHOUSE, CHATHAM COUNTY

Tybee Island is a barrier island and a small city located eighteen miles east of the city of Savannah. The island is considered the easternmost tip of Georgia. Longtime residents still refer to Tybee Island as Savannah Beach. I collected many old postcards from the 1950s and 1960s from Savannah Beach before I realized it was Tybee Island. The island is only 3.2 square miles in size and has a resident population around three thousand.

The Tybee Island Lighthouse, located on the northeast end of Tybee Island, is one of only seven surviving colonial-era lighthouse towers. Portions of the tower structure date to 1773, including the bottom 60 feet of the lighthouse. The lighthouse is 154 feet tall and equipped with a first-order Fresnel lens. The top 94 feet of the lighthouse was added in 1867. The lighthouse keeper's residence was built in 1885.

The lighthouse sits within the historic footprint of Fort Screven, which was a commissioned fort established for coastal defense in 1899. General of the Army George C. Marshall was one of the former commanding officers. There is very little remaining of the existing fort today, but beach fortifications have been preserved and house a museum.

I first saw the lighthouse in 2002, when the City of Tybee Island hired my firm to do a parking analysis for the island and a master plan for the South Beach commercial district. The lighthouse sits on the northwestern end of the island and watches over the shipping channel to the Port of Savannah.

TYBEE ISLAND LIGHTHOUSE

South Georgia

Jekyll Island Gatehouse, Glynn County

The history of Jekyll Island is one of the most interesting stories associated with the Georgia coast. The semitropical island was a hunting grounds for Indians, the site of a Spanish mission, a French-owned plantation and a winter retreat for northern industrialists. It is believed that the Spanish established a mission on the island of "Ospo" (Jekyll Island) around 1566. In 1680, British from Charleston led an attack on the mission. In 1733, General James Edward Oglethorpe founded the colony of Georgia. He renamed Ospo for his friend Sir Joseph Jekyll, who made a sizeable donation toward Oglethorpe's expedition. At that time, part of the island was cleared and planted in hops and grain to support Georgia's first brewery, located on the river side of the island. Tabby ruins on the island are believed to be the ruins of the home of Major William Horton, who was in charge of the plantation. In the late 1790s, a French family by the name of du Bignon bought the island and lived there for almost one hundred years. The slave ship *Wanderer* secretly landed a cargo of enslaved people on the island in 1858. This is known to be the last shipment of human cargo ever brought to America. In the 1880s, a group of northern industrialists began looking for a private winter resort that would have a healthy climate and good weather during the season. In 1886, Jekyll Island was bought from John Eugene du Bignon for $125,000.

To get to Jekyll Island, a visitor must pass a pair of flanking gatehouses that mark the entrance to the Jekyll Island Causeway. The causeway, now known as Downing Musgrove Causeway (Ga 520), was built by the state to provide access to the once exclusive private club. It is by far one of my favorite places to visit in Georgia. Built in the 1960s, the gatehouses stand sentinel over that bygone era.

Jekyll Island Club Hotel, Glynn County

Jekyll Island is a barrier island and one of the "Golden Isles" that line the Georgia coast. Jekyll Island is larger than Tybee Island at 10.5 square miles. The Jekyll Island Club Hotel is part of a 240-acre National Register Historic District designated in 1978. The district includes thirty-three buildings from the late nineteenth and early twentieth centuries, including elegant mansions or "cottages" built by the wealthy club members.

The Jekyll Island Club, a luxury resort hotel, was originally built as a clubhouse for a private hunting and recreational club. Members of the club included notable wealthy families such as the Rockefellers, Morgans and Vanderbilts. Other well-known families associated with the island include Pulitzer, Roosevelt, Astor, Goodyear and Macy. The original structure, including the tower, was completed in 1888. During World War II, the U.S. government ordered the island evacuated for security purposes. After the war, in 1947, the State of Georgia bought the island for $675,000. Initially a

South Georgia

state park, Jekyll Island was turned over to the Jekyll Island Authority in 1950. The clubhouse and surrounding cottages were designated a National Historic Landmark in 1978.

I first visited the old clubhouse on a college field trip around 1980. At that time, the clubhouse was closed pending renovation. It reopened following renovation in 1987. It is a thrill today to stay at the hotel, which is sprinkled with historic photos from the bygone era of those early robber barons that vacationed on the island.

Tabby Sugar Works, Camden County

Tabby is a type of building material used along the Georgia coast from the late 1500s to the 1850s. The Spanish are credited with bringing the use of tabby to the New World and used it extensively in Florida. Tabby in Georgia is made from equal parts lime, water, sand, oyster shells and ash. The tabby mixture can be poured like concrete into forms for walls, foundations, floors and columns. Tabby dries hard like concrete to a grayish-white color. General James Oglethorpe advocated the use of tabby in the 1700s because of the abundance of oyster shells found in Indian shell mounds. Tabby is best used with an exterior stucco finish. Several of the historic cottages in the Jekyll Island historic district were made using tabby. I first heard of tabby when I was interviewing a candidate for a position with our firm in the late 1980s. She presented a paper she had written in college on the use of tabby in Georgia.

My team was hired to develop a Joint Land Use Study for Camden County and the King's Bay Naval Submarine Base around 2012. Up until that time, I had not spent any time in the southeast corner of Georgia below Jekyll Island and Brunswick. Camden County and St. Mary's are a beautiful community with some unusual historical remnants, such as the ruins of the old tabby sugar plantation built by John Houston McIntosh. McIntosh was a former governor of Florida and a general who served in the Seminole War in 1818. The ruins date from the early 1820s after McIntosh moved to Camden County. Sugar was an important cash crop in the late 1700s and early 1800s. Georgia's coastal climate suited the growing of sugarcane. The Tabby Sugar Works are located off of Charlie Smith Sr. Highway (SR40), six miles north of St. Mary's and across the street from the entrance into the Naval Submarine Base Kings Bay.

Plant Park Fountain, Waycross, Ware County

Waycross is the county seat of Ware County. Waycross was incorporated in 1873 and gets its name as a railroad junction where six different railroads meet. Currently, CSX Railroad operates a large classification yard in Waycross. Downtown Waycross is only a few miles north of the Okefenokee National Wildlife Refuge. The wildlife refuge is a 400,000-acre refuge located in Charlton, Ware and Clinch Counties. The refuge was established in 1937 to protect the Okefenokee Swamp. Okefenokee is an Indian word meaning "trembling earth."

The Plant Park fountain was abandoned, rusting and missing pieces when I first saw it in the early 1990s. I was preparing a plan for the City of Waycross at that time and recommended that the park and fountain be refurbished to be used as a trailhead for future bicycle and walking trails. Thanks to a federal grant, the city was able to hire our firm to redesign the park and refurbish the fountain. The original fountain was cast by Robinson Iron (an Alabama Company) more than one hundred years ago.

South Georgia

The company is still in business today and was able to recast the missing pieces as part of the restoration.

At the time I was working with the city, we promoted a policy to connect the city to the north entrance to the wildlife refuge. I vividly remember my first visit to the visitor facilities at the north entrance. At that time, alligators roamed freely around the buildings, trails and parking. They were purportedly fed by the staff and docile. We commonly walked within two to three feet of full-grown alligators. We were told to stay away from the small or baby alligators in case the mother might be nearby.

Tift Theater, Tifton, Tift County

In February 1937, the Tift opened with its premiere performance of *Pennies from Heaven*. For the next fifty years, the theater delighted Tifton with stars of the silver screen in blockbuster releases and theatrical productions. The theater saw three wars come and go before it went dark in 1987.

The community rallied to support the effort to refurbish the historic Tift Theater. Citizens and businesses donated one-third of the funds needed to refurbish the building. The building reopened in the mid-1990s with a fundraising gala organized by Tifton's Olympic Committee. The theater has 612 seats and is adorned with circus-themed accents originally created by a Ringling Brothers artist.

The Modernistic or Art Deco theater sports signature elements of design from the 1930s. The ornamentation is predominantly rectilinear, with geometric curves playing a secondary role. Chevrons or zigzags are employed on the sign. Verticality is stressed with a colored glass veneer in contrasting polychromatic colors. The vertical elements of the façade do not stop under a protruding cornice. The smooth geometric shapes that form the building ornament are strongly influenced by modern artistic movements such as cubism.

Fulwood Park, Tifton, Tift County

The city of Tifton is located approximately 175 miles south of Atlanta and just east of Interstate 75. Tifton is the county seat of Tift County. Tifton was founded in 1872 as a railroad community and named for Henry H. Tift, who owned and operated a local sawmill. Norfolk-Southern Freight Railway currently runs through Tifton. Passenger rail services ended in 1970. The downtown commercial historic district is listed in the National Register of Historic Places.

In the 1990s, our firm was retained to develop gateway landscape plans for the seven Interstate 75 interchanges in the city of Tifton. In 2012, our firm continued work with the city in the development of sidewalk and parking improvements in the historic downtown.

I had the opportunity to work with my wife on a wayfinding signage study for the City of Tifton. One of the goals was to direct visitors to local landmarks. Fulwood Park is considered a local landmark and sits on approximately thirty beautifully landscaped acres just a few minutes' walk from downtown. Established in 1916, the park is named for one of the pioneer families in Tift County. The stone arch is dated 1934 and reminiscent of the stonework built by the CCC in the 1930s.

Radium Springs Gazebo, Albany, Dougherty County

Radium springs is a unique bubbling blue hole spring that is considered one of the Seven Natural Wonders of Georgia. The area surrounding the springs was developed in the 1920s to include a golf course, casino and assorted resort-style accommodations. The springs attracted northern travelers on their way to Florida seeking the health benefits of the springs. The springs and the surrounding land were originally purchased and developed by Barron G. Collier in 1925.

ABANDONED GAZEBO
RADIUM SPRINGS
ALBANY, GEORGIA

The Radium Country Club and Golf Course was built in 1927 and designed by golf course architect John Law Kerr. On June 23, 1927, a golf exhibition took place between the great Georgia golfer Bobby Jones and the Australian "trick shot" specialist Joe Kirkwood. Kirkwood won the exhibition by five strokes. Later the same year, Bobby Jones won the British Open with Joe Kirkwood finishing in fourth, six strokes back. The springs resort and spa closed toward the end of the Great Depression in 1939. A group of local investors purchased the casino resort in 1944. Since that time, the springs have experienced various openings and closings. In 1994 and 1998, there were catastrophic floods that led to the eventual demolition of the casino building and the permanent closure of the golf course.

I have been working with Dougherty County for twenty years on the restoration and preservation of portions of the springs. The concrete and plaster gazebo ruins are unique in their form and construction. Probably built in the 1930s, the gazebo ruins are now a focal point near the entry into newly created gardens. In 2017, the gazebo was damaged by a severe tornado that killed five people in the area. I designed a memorial to the storm victims that was completed in 2020 along with repairs to the gazebo.

Radium Springs Ticket Booth, Dougherty County

Radium Springs is the largest natural spring in Georgia and located a few miles south of the city of Albany on the east side of the Flint River. The aqua blue spring water has trace amounts of radium and a constant water temperature of sixty-eight degrees. The spring produces an average of seventy thousand gallons per minute that flows down a spring run and empties into the Flint River.

The ticket booth at Radium Springs is a remnant of a bygone era in Albany, Georgia. It is a unique piece of architecture that I cannot decide whether or not is attractive. To the residents of Albany and Dougherty County, it was the passageway into the Radium Springs swimming hole, casino and spa developed in the 1920s. The constant sixty-eight-degree water must have felt like heaven for swimmers escaping the heat of the summer in South Georgia.

ABANDONED ENTRANCE GATE
RADIUM SPRINGS
ALBANY, GEORGIA

The site has been flooded many times and was eventually closed. The county purchased the site and retained my firm in 2002 to do a master plan for the ninety acres surrounding the springs. As part of our work, we preserved the ticket booth as a unique element to the new public gardens designed by my firm. Our work was featured in a WSB television special on Radium Springs titled *Georgia's Hidden Treasures*. We updated the plan in 2019, as the county is hoping to bring back swimming for area residents.

Gateway Arch, Dougherty County/Mitchell County

Old Dixie Highway in Dougherty County follows the Flint River and was a major roadway connector to Florida long before there were interstate highways. Georgia Power Company operates a large power plant adjacent

South Georgia

to the old roadway near the boundary with Mitchell County. I was working with Dougherty County to assess damage caused by a series of tornados in 2017. While documenting the existing land uses in the area, I stumbled across this amazing cast concrete arch erected over the roadway. There are no markings or dates on the gateway arch, but my guess is that it was built post–World War II as America mobilized after the war.

In 2018, our firm was retained to assist the county in the development of a recovery plan from tornados that severely damaged the area in 2017. As part of that process, we hosted a public open house in the area. One of the African American senior citizens from the area shared with me a story about the Dixie Highway. When he was a youth, he used to pick southern magnolia blossoms and give them to motorists heading to Florida. Northern tourists likely had never seen the giant blossoms of the magnolia, which can be as large as twelve inches across. He would use the tip money to go to the local neighborhood store and buy a Coca-Cola.

GATEWAY ARCH ON THE DIXIE HIGHWAY
DOUGHERTY COUNTY / MITCHELL COUNTY

3
CENTRAL GEORGIA

I find joy and meaning in an artist's interpretation of an idea.
—*Therese Huffman*

I moved to Georgia in 1984 and settled in Augusta. At that time, there was abundant talk about building a "developmental" highway system across Georgia as a catalyst for economic development under Governor Joe Frank Harris. A key component of that system was a "Fall Line Highway" that would link Augusta, Macon and Columbus. The "fall line" in Georgia is the transition from the ancient coastal sea of the Coastal Plain as it becomes the rolling hills of the Piedmont. The fall line cities occur in this transition zone, where rocky shoals in the rivers and landscape give way to the sands of the coastal plain.

As such, the fall line cities contain a terrific collection of unique historic buildings and sites. They each played a critical role in industrial production before and after the Civil War. Water from the Savannah River was channelized to provide power in Augusta, water from the Ocmulgee River was used to power production in Macon and water from the Chattahoochee River in Columbus was diverted to support the mills along the river.

In this section are a few of the unique treasures associated with these cities and others near the fall line. When I first moved to Augusta, I enjoyed hiking along the Augusta Canal and exploring the bottom when it was drained in the summer for maintenance. I assembled a nice collection of historic glass bottles I had picked up from the bottom of the canal. Augusta's historic

Woodrow Wilson House was a local hair salon at the time I lived in the city. Included in this section is a sketch of the last freshwater automobile ferry, an icehouse, a smokehouse, an opera house and the oldest jail in Georgia. Central Georgia was also the home of three Georgia capitals—Augusta, Louisville and Milledgeville—before Atlanta. This section also includes sketches from Georgia College and State University and Mercer University. I have included a sketch of the Chapel at Callaway Gardens to pay homage to one of the state's landscape treasures. I first visited the gardens in the late 1970s to go horseback riding with a friend from Auburn University.

Project Notes

By far my favorite project in Central Georgia was the design and construction of Thiele Memorial Park in Sandersville. I met the city manager when she stopped to take a look at my sketch of the Concord Covered Bridge that was being raffled as part of our firm's trade show exhibit. At that time, we discussed the city's desire to have a plan prepared for some vacant land downtown and the need to spruce up the city streets. Eventually, the vacant land became the Memorial Park. The park was named after a longtime community leader, Paul F. Thiele. Thiele was the president of Thiele Kaolin, which is a major local industry. Kaolin is a platy, white clay that is chemically inert and nonabrasive. It is distinguished from other clays by its fine particle size and pure white coloring. The Kaolin "Belt" is located across nine counties on the edge of the ancient ocean between Columbus and Augusta. Kaolin deposits are primarily found in the United States in Central Georgia on the fall line between Augusta and Macon. The first mining of Kaolin in Georgia was in McIntyre, Georgia, in 1908.

Washington County is one of the main fall line counties that provides source Kaolin. Kaolin clay is used in paper, paint, rubber, cable insulation, specialty films, medicines, plastics, ceramics, toothpaste, cosmetics and more. The primary use of Kaolin (approximately 50 percent) is for paper coating. Glossy paper or "clay-coated" paper achieves the gloss through the use of Kaolin.

The park design features an unusual twenty-eight-foot bell tower and three wrought-iron gateway arches. The design for the bell tower was inspired by the carillon located at Stone Mountain Park, originally designed for the 1964 World's Fair in New York. The wrought-iron arches are my own unique design, but they were built by the well-known Atlanta artist and ironsmith Andrew Crawford.

Other projects in the region that I enjoyed working on include the renovation and landscape for the Woodrow Wilson House in Augusta and the feasibility study for the reuse or preservation of the last freshwater automobile ferry in Georgia across the Flint River.

LIST OF ILLUSTRATIONS

49. Head Gates for the Augusta Canal, Columbia County
50. Augusta Canal at Thirteenth Street, Augusta, Richmond County
51. Woodrow Wilson House, Augusta, Richmond County
52. The Graves Barn, Sparta, Hancock County
53. Oldest Jail in Georgia, Warthen, Washington County
54. Cotton Gin, Hamburg State Park, Washington County
55. Icehouse, Sandersville, Washington County
56. Smokehouse, Bulloch County
57. Georgia College and State University, Milledgeville, Baldwin County
58. Gateway to the Old Capitol Building, Milledgeville, Baldwin County
59. Administration Building, Mercer University, Macon, Bibb County
60. Entry Gate at Luther Williams Field, Macon, Bibb County
61. The Chapel at Callaway Gardens, Harris County
62. Visitor's Center, FDR State Park, Pine Mountain, Harris County
63. Little White House, Warm Springs, Meriwether County
64. Springer Opera House, Columbus, Muscogee County
65. Flint River Ferry, Macon County
66. The Spring House at Indian Springs State Park, Butts County

HEAD GATES FOR THE AUGUSTA CANAL, COLUMBIA COUNTY

I first visited the head gates in 1984 as part of my exploration of the entire Augusta Canal system. At that time, the head gates were located at the end of a dirt road and included a caretaker's residence, a Victorian dance pavilion and a covered barbecue pit. All of the structures were in declining condition.

A Scenic Georgia Sketchbook

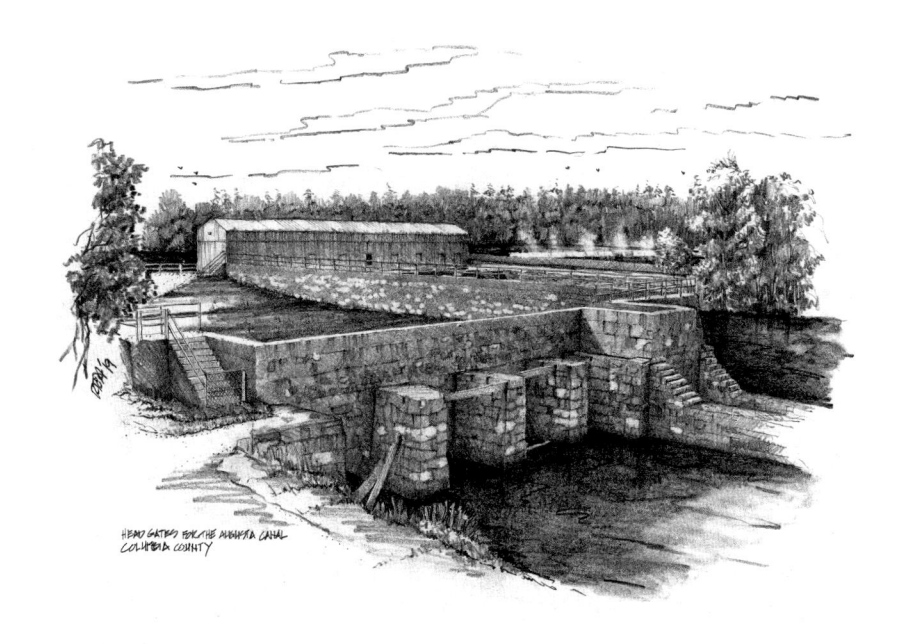

The construction of the Augusta Canal head gates and locks occurred in three phases: the building of the original head gates and lock in 1846 (in the foreground of the sketch), the addition of the 1874–75 head gates and lock (middle of the sketch) and a Works Progress Administration (WPA) revitalization project in the 1930s. John Edgar Thomson selected the site for the head gates in 1844, but the foundation was not laid until February 1846. The first water flowed through the gates on November 23, 1846, and three months later, the first barge full of cotton entered the lock.

The present configuration of locks was the result of the 1872–75 enlargement of the canal. Atop the site of the original cribwork dam, a rubble abutment was extended twenty-two and a half feet from the 1846 head gates and lock to the newer complex. The locks constitute the major difference between the two complexes. The old lock had a drop gate, which limited the height of boats using the canal, while the new lock had obstructing swing gates. A dam and spillway extend from the bulkhead across the Savannah River.

Today, the site has been restored, and the county has built a large conference and meeting facility adjacent. The caretaker's residence and surrounding areas have been expanded into a trailhead with trailhead parking to support boating and bicycling along the canal.

Central Georgia

Augusta Canal at Thirteenth Street, Augusta, Richmond County

I first saw the Augusta Canal in the early 1980s when I moved to Augusta. The Augusta Canal includes three levels and was originally constructed in 1845–46 and enlarged in 1874–77. The first level reaches eight and a half miles from the head gate structures into downtown Augusta. The head gates of the canal are on the Savannah River in Columbia County. The second and third levels take several paths through the city before returning to the Savannah River for a total length of thirteen and a half miles. The Augusta Canal has been added to the National Register of Historic Places and is now part of a National Heritage Area/Historic Augusta Canal and Industrial District. The city formed an authority, and there are walking trails, a museum and boat tours available on the canal.

The Thirteenth Street head gates, constructed in 1910, still perform the original function of maintaining the height and flow of the canal's first level while allowing excess water to pass on to the second level. The five metal gates are raised vertically, each by its own hand-operated worm gearing mechanism. Canal water flows seven miles from the head gates and locks to Thirteenth Street. Mills along the first level of the canal had a waterfall of thirty-three feet to the Savannah River or a fall of eighteen feet to the second level of the canal. Industries along the second level had a fall of thirteen feet to the third level. Three existing mills still use canal water to power hydroelectric plants.

The canal's chief engineer, C.O. Stanford, is credited with designing the 1846 lock and head gates. Henry H. Cumming, an Augusta native, spearheaded the construction, envisioning that Augusta could one day become "the Lowell [Massachusetts] of the South." The canal was also the location of the Confederate States Powder Works.

Woodrow Wilson House, Augusta, Richmond County

Built in 1859, the Woodrow Wilson House served as the manse for the First Presbyterian Church across the street. Woodrow Wilson's father was the minister for the church from 1860 to 1872. Woodrow Wilson, born in 1856, spent these critical formative years in Augusta. Next door to this house is the home of his childhood playmate who became an associate justice to the United States Supreme Court, Joseph Rucker Lamar.

When I lived in Augusta in the early 1980s, the house had fallen into disrepair, and a portion of it was used as a beauty salon. In the late 1990s, my firm was hired to help with the renovation of the house. We worked closely with a preservation architect, while we focused on the site, the gardens, parking and connections to the adjacent chief justice's house, which now serves as the visitor center for the historic house and the home of Historic Augusta Inc. The house is located on the corner of Telfair and Seventh Streets. The house is located only one block from some of the most unique and historic properties in Augusta, including the original Medical College (circa 1835), the Gertrude Herbert Institute of Art (circa 1818) and the original building for Richmond Academy (circa 1857). All four buildings represent just a portion of the rich architectural heritage that can be found in Augusta.

The Graves Barn, Sparta, Hancock County

Located one block south of Broad Street and a couple of blocks from the Hancock County Courthouse, the Graves barn sits on an isolated land parcel with a sign indicating the barn dates from 1890. The barn features some unique woodwork above the doors and in the gables. I was passing through Sparta on my way to Sandersville. I took a couple of extra minutes to wander off the main road and spotted the barn. I stopped to take pictures and do a few quick sketches.

Sparta is one of the most unique cities in Georgia. Sparta became the county seat for the newly formed Hancock County in 1795. Hancock County was formed from a portion of Greene and Washington Counties. Sparta became chartered in 1803 and was the first town in Georgia developed with four streets running into the center of the courthouse square rather than to the sides. As such, future cities developed in this pattern in Georgia are referred to as having followed the Sparta plan. The Hancock County Courthouse, which sits adjacent to the courthouse square, is one of the finest in Georgia. The building burned in 2014. The exterior walls were saved, and the courthouse was rebuilt to match the original.

Oldest Jail in Georgia, Warthen, Washington County

I have passed through Warthen many times on my way to see clients in Sandersville. There is a sign along Highway 15 that calls out the "Oldest Jail in Georgia." On one of my trips, I decided to go see it for myself and was pleasantly surprised to find this unique and wonderful piece of architecture nestled along an abandoned railroad track. Designated as a historic site, the old jail was purportedly used to hold Vice President Aaron Burr overnight on his journey to Richmond, Virginia, to stand trial for treason. The simple one-room log structure was built somewhere around 1783–93. It is considered Washington County's first jail and is located in the heart of the Warthen Historic District.

Aaron Burr served as vice president under Thomas Jefferson (1801–5). He also served in the Continental army during the American Revolution, was elected to the state assembly in New York and served as a U.S. senator from New York (1791–97). He is remembered for shooting to death his political rival Alexander Hamilton in a duel in 1804. He never went to trial for the illegal duel; however, he was eventually arrested for treason in 1807. Burr hoped to help Mexico overthrow Spanish power, which was a violation of the Neutrality Act of 1794. He was charged with treason and intercepted in Alabama as he fled toward Spanish Florida. He was brought to trial in

Central Georgia

Richmond, Virginia, where he was acquitted. Burr lived a self-imposed exile in England from 1808 to 1812 before returning to the United States to live out the remainder of his life in New York.

Cotton Gin, Hamburg State Park, Washington County

Hamburg State Park is located on the site of the Gilmore brothers' mill, dam and cotton gin built in 1921–22. Prior to the Gilmore brothers, one of the first mills in Washington County was built by the Warthen family about seventy-five feet upstream from the present mill and cotton gin between 1790 and 1810. The mill and the surrounding property on the Little Ogeechee River changed hands multiple times until it was eventually sold to the State of Georgia in 1968. The Hamburg Mill and the surrounding properties were named by the Warthen family after the great market in Hamburg, South Carolina, just across the river from Augusta, Georgia.

In 1794, Eli Whitney received a patent for his cotton gin, which separated cotton from its sticky seeds. This machine dramatically decreased the amount of labor involved in cotton production. This productivity led to the spread of cotton as a profitable cash crop across the southern United States. *Gin* is short for "engine." Although Eli Whitney was born in Massachusetts, following his graduation from Yale College, he visited Georgia at the request of Catharine Littlefield Greene, the widow of Revolutionary War hero Nathaniel Greene. Catharine Greene's Plantation, Mulberry Grove, was located in Chatham County outside of Savannah. While staying at Mulberry Grove, Whitney developed a model machine to remove seeds from cotton. The cotton gin transformed southern agriculture. Cotton exports from the United States jumped from 500,000 pounds in 1793 to 93 million pounds by 1810.

Cottonseed is an important byproduct from the ginning process. Farmers used cottonseed to produce the next year's crop. Vegetable oils and margarine are other common uses for cottonseed. After the seed was cleaned, it was blown through metal flues into a hopper and dumped into wagons parked below the hopper.

Central Georgia

ICEHOUSE, SANDERSVILLE, WASHINGTON COUNTY

Icehouses were big business before refrigeration. Ice was shipped from New England, packed in sawdust and sent to ports like Savannah and Brunswick. The ice was delivered and stored in icehouses. Private icehouses were typically roof-covered deep cellars or brick-lined pits up to ten to fifteen feet deep. The ice could keep until the next season's delivery. Commercial icehouses are uncommon today, but back during the early twentieth century, an icehouse was a center of activity where citizens could buy ice, cold beer and groceries. Icehouses were the precursor to today's convenience stores. The well-known local Georgia convenience store chain of Majik Markets began as icehouses, originally founded as the Atlantic Ice and Coal Company in Atlanta.

I do not know the history of this icehouse in Sandersville. It is located on Gilmore Street, which was the center for African American commerce in the city in the early twentieth century. The roof awnings are supported with ice tongs. One of the most unique building details I have seen in my travels around Georgia and a clear indicator of the purpose of the building, the cornerstone includes the following information: "Municipal Ice Plant 1930, Water and Light Commission, W.H. Smith, Chr., Geo. W. Gilmore, M.L. Cross."

A Scenic Georgia Sketchbook

Smokehouse, Bulloch County

A smokehouse is a building where meat is cured with smoke. The cured meat is stored in the structure, usually hanging from rafters or packed in salt. Smokehouses were popular prior to the widespread use of electricity and freezers. This smokehouse in Bulloch County is located near what will become an extension of a trail running between Statesboro and Brooklet. I spotted the smokehouse during a site investigation for the trail routing. The building has several signature components of a smokehouse, including the circular wall vents on the side. The smokers would be located outside the building and the smoke fed through the side walls. The covered awning on the front face was for wood storage, and the metal doors were used to secure the building to prevent theft. There are no windows, and the roof has a small but pronounced ridge vent. I have seen many smaller wooden smokehouses from the nineteenth century, but this particular building is much later based on the type of brick masonry block that was used for construction.

At one time, Bulloch County was the largest producer of "Sea Island" cotton in the world. Sea Island cotton is difficult to grow but more valuable than other varieties because of its long fibers. A bale of Sea Island cotton was worth more than twice the price of a bale of ordinary cotton. In the early years of the 1900s, the boll weevil, native to Central America, made its way from Texas to Georgia. The insect decimated cotton crops, resulting in reduced production by more than 50 percent in ten years. It was not until a successful program to eradicate the weevil was begun in 1987 that cotton again became a viable crop in Georgia.

Georgia College and State University, Milledgeville, Baldwin County

Located on the southeast corner of the quadrangle at GCSU, the Victorian clock tower sits on top of the former Baldwin County courthouse. Built in 1887 for the cost of $25,000, the clock tower anchors the main quadrangle like so many towers across college campuses in the South. The clocktower is part of a large historic district comprising more than a dozen buildings listed in the National Register of Historic Places.

Largely through the effort of William Y. Atkinson and Julia Flisch, the Georgia Normal and Industrial College was founded in 1889 with J. Harris Chappell as the first president. Originally chartered as a two-year college emphasizing teacher training and business, it became a four-year degree-granting institution in 1917 and included a liberal arts program. The name was changed in 1922 to the Georgia State College for Women and in 1961 to the Women's College of Georgia. In 1967, the Women's College became coeducational, and the name was changed to Georgia College. In 1996, the name was changed to Georgia College and State University.

Today GCSU is part of the University System of Georgia and is a coed liberal arts college under the name Georgia College and State University. Georgia College and State

University serves more than 6,600 undergraduate and graduate students in four colleges: the College of Arts and Sciences, the J. Whitney Bunting College of Business, the John H. Lounsbury College of Education and the College of Health Science.

My son, Russell, attended GCSU and graduated in 2012. I sketched the tower and gave it to him as a Christmas present and keepsake.

GATEWAY TO THE OLD CAPITOL BUILDING, MILLEDGEVILLE, BALDWIN COUNTY

Milledgeville served as the state capital from 1804 to 1868. The Georgia Military College currently occupies the site of the former capitol. Originally founded as the Middle Georgia Military and Agricultural College in 1879, the college occupied the capitol building, which was vacated when the capital moved to Atlanta in 1868. The original capitol was built in 1805 with $60,000 appropriated by the state legislature. Revolutionary War hero the Marquis de Lafayette visited the statehouse in 1825. Architect Henry Hamilton Fulton oversaw the expansion of the building from 1827 to 1834. It was at this location that the succession convention met on January 16,

1861, and after three days of debate passed the Secession Act. The building was occupied by Sherman on his March to the Sea in 1864. Following renovation due to damage caused by Sherman's forces, the building briefly served as the county courthouse. Fire almost totally destroyed the building in 1941. The exterior walls were all that was left standing. It was restored by the Georgia Military College.

The college opened for classes in 1880 with 219 students in grades 1–12. The college was renamed the Georgia Military College in 1900. Currently, the college locally enrolls around 20,00 students in middle school, high school, junior college and military junior college. Including remote campuses, the college's total enrollment is approximately 14,000 students.

The gate was built around 1867. It was designed and construction supervised by Federal army colonel B.W. Froebel.

Administration Building, Mercer University, Macon, Bibb County

The R. Kirby Godsey administration building stands sentinel over the campus of Mercer University in Macon. The building is named after the seventeenth president of the university, who served from July 1979 until June 2006. The building is listed in the National Register of Historic Places and was erected in the 1870s after the university, which was founded in 1838, moved to Macon from Penfield, Georgia, in 1871. The completed construction cost was $100,000. I was told by a former alumnus that the tower originally was a clock tower. It is the tallest structure on campus.

Initially a male preparatory school named Mercer Institute, the institution was founded by Georgia Baptists and named for Jesse Mercer, a prominent Baptist leader. The school originally included a farm and two hewed log cabins valued at approximately $1,935 in Penfield, Georgia. Enrollment for the first term was thirty-nine students, tuition was $35 and boarding was provided for $8 per month. Mercer Institute became Mercer University in 1838, and the first college class graduated in 1841. Mercer University is the only college in Georgia to remain open during the Civil War.

Mercer University played the University of Georgia in the first college football game in the state of Georgia in January 1892. Georgia won 50–0. Mercer University also played the first football game ever by the Georgia Tech Yellow Jackets. Mercer University won that game 12–6 in the fall of 1892.

Today, Mercer University is a private university that enrolls approximately 8,600 students in twelve colleges and schools: liberal arts, business, engineering, education, music, law, theology, medicine, nursing, continuing and professional studies and health professions.

Entry Gate at Luther Williams Field, Macon, Bibb County

Located in Central City Park in downtown Macon, Luther Williams Field was built in 1929 and is listed in the National Register of Historic Places. The structure was designed by the architect Curran R. Ellis, and the engineer was Watson Walker. It is named for the Macon mayor who championed building the stadium. The original covered grandstand is still in place. A variety of minor league baseball teams have called the stadium home, including the Macon Peaches (1926–1983 and 2003), the Macon Dodgers (1956–1960), the Macon Pirates (1984–1987), the Macon Braves (1991–2002), the Macon Pinetoppers (2010), the Macon Blue Storm (2011–2012) and the Macon Bacon (2018–to the present). The stadium has a seating capacity of three thousand. The field dimensions are 338 feet to left field, 402 feet to center field and 338 feet to right field. Several well-known major-league baseball players played at the stadium including Pete Rose ('62), Tony Perez ('63), Vince Coleman ('83), Chipper Jones ('91), Jermaine Dye ('94) and Andruw Jones ('95).

Central City Park is Macon's oldest and largest city park. The park was built in 1828, influenced by Dr. Ambrose Baber, who recommended that park land be set aside along the Ocmulgee River for the health of the city. There is a speaker's stand gazebo located in the park that was built in 1871 and is also listed on the National Register of Historic Places. Jefferson Davis, president of the Confederacy, addressed veterans of the Civil War from the speaker's stand in 1887.

The Chapel at Callaway Gardens, Harris County

I first visited Callaway Gardens when I was in college in the 1970s. I saw the Chapel (IDA Cason Callaway Memorial Chapel) and was immediately moved by its beauty. Coincidentally, Callaway Gardens was a client for the first firm I worked with in Atlanta. The designer of the chapel, which dates from the 1960s, no longer worked for the firm, but I would pull the original drawings and sketches from the file and admire the work. The chapel was designed by the architect Robert Moulthrup. Moulthrup is well known for his dramatic work with turned wooden bowls.

Callaway Resort & Gardens is located in the southern foothills of the Appalachian Mountains. The gardens were developed by Cason and Virginia Callaway. Cason Callaway was president of Callaway Mills in nearby LaGrange. The Callaways frequently picnicked with friends in

Blue Springs near Hamilton. Cason discovered the rare plumleaf azalea growing near Blue Springs and bought 2,500 acres that included the wild-growing azalea in 1930. Eventually, the Callaways grew the acreage to include 40,000 acres. Cason and Virginia began creating the gardens in 1949 and eventually deeded the land to the Ida Cason Callaway Foundation. Ida Cason Callaway was the sister-in-law of Cason Callaway. The gardens were first opened to the public in 1952. Today the resort and gardens include a hotel and conference center, lodge and spa, golf courses, lake, the Cecil B. Day Butterfly Center, a network of bicycle trails, the chapel and cottages.

Visitor's Center, FDR State Park, Pine Mountain, Harris County

Pine Mountain, in Harris County, is one of the prettiest parts of Georgia. The FDR State Park Visitor's Center sits on top of Pine Mountain with a commanding view across the valley below. The stone building was constructed

Central Georgia

by the Civilian Conservation Corps during the Great Depression of the 1930s. The craftsmanship in rock and stone that is associated with the CCC is very clearly and beautifully represented in the visitor's center.

F.D. Roosevelt State Park originally was sitting in Creek Indian Territory. The Creeks lost the land by treaty in 1825–26. F.D. Roosevelt State Park is Georgia's largest state park at 9,049 acres. There are more than 40 miles of trails, including the 23-mile Pine Mountain Trail. Dowdell's Knob is where Franklin Roosevelt sometimes picnicked and pondered world affairs. A life-size sculpture marks the spot, which is now preserved as an overlook within the park.

Located nearby F.D. Roosevelt State Park is Warm Springs Village. President Roosevelt brought national attention to Warm Springs, when, in 1924, he visited the town's naturally heated mineral springs–fed pools for treatment for his polio-related paralysis. The warm springs maintains a constant eighty-eight-degree temperature year-round and flows at approximately nine hundred gallons per minute. Georgia State Parks has refurbished the pools, which include a touch pool for visitors to feel the actual warm water with an interpretive exhibit that tells the story of polio and its virtual eradication. Roosevelt founded the Roosevelt Warm

Visitor's Center @ Roosevelt State Park, Pine Mountain

Springs Institute in 1927 as a polio rehabilitation facility that today focuses on empowering people with disabilities through vocational rehabilitation programs. Warm Springs Village is the historic commercial center for the area and has an array of specialty shops, restaurants and hotels.

LITTLE WHITE HOUSE, WARM SPRINGS, MERIWETHER COUNTY

The Little White House was Franklin Delano Roosevelt's Georgia getaway. While searching for a place to recover after he was stricken with polio in the early 1920s, Roosevelt and his family traveled to Warm Springs (twelve miles from the Little White House). He was fond of the community of Warm Springs and the namesake warm water springs. He sought therapy and relief from the polio that affected the use of his legs. He spent so much time in Warm Springs that he built a beautiful small home referred to as the Little White House. FDR passed away in 1945 after suffering from a stroke while posing for a portrait in the Little White House, which is now a state-operated historic site. The unfinished portrait is located in a museum on the grounds, which also includes exhibits such as FDR's 1938 Ford Convertible with hand controls, his stagecoach and recordings of his "fireside chats," which were broadcast nationally over the radio. The house is beautifully preserved and furnished as it was during FDR's time. The garage building and the companion cottage are unique architectural treasures that flank the approach to the house.

SPRINGER OPERA HOUSE, COLUMBUS, MUSCOGEE COUNTY

At the time it was built in 1871, the Springer Opera House quickly gained the reputation as the finest theater between New Orleans and New York. Francis Joseph Springer, originally of the Alsace region in Europe, designed and built the opera house. The Springer's forty-foot-deep stage allowed for a wide variety of different shows of every description.

The Springer played host to many well-known actors, musicians and politicians. Edwin Booth played Hamlet on February 15, 1876, on his first southern tour after the war. "Blind Tom" Bethune, the African American musical prodigy born near Columbus, performed here often. Oscar Wilde and William Jennings Bryan lectured there; John L. Sullivan, the world champion, gave a boxing exhibition; and Mrs. John (Louisa Lane) Drew, grandmother of the Barrymores, starred in *She Stoops to Conquer*. John Philip Sousa's band performed at the Springer, as did Will Rogers. In 1928, Franklin Delano Roosevelt delivered a "Happy Warrior" speech on behalf of presidential nominee Al Smith.

In 1902, the Springer was completely renovated and continued as a theater until the Great Depression. At that time, it became a movie house and eventually was closed in 1959 and threatened with demolition in 1964. The Columbus Little Theater Opera House Trustees was formed to prevent its destruction. On October 6, 1965, the theater reopened and in 1998–99 underwent a $12 million renovation. The Springer is the oldest professional theater in Georgia and one of only seven theaters in the United States designated as a National Historic Landmark.

Flint River Ferry, Macon County

Ferries provided river crossing when there were no bridges and the rivers ran too high to be forded. Most ferries date from the early 1800s, but the heyday for ferries was the late nineteenth century. Some were pulled by horses, but most were operated by a system of pullies and cables. Most were also privately owned. When the Georgia Highway Department took over the state's roadway system in the 1920s, the ferries on state roads were purchased and the tolls abolished. There were at least four known ferries in Macon County across the Flint River.

In the late 1980s, the Flint River Ferry was the last operating freshwater automobile ferry in Georgia. It was going to be replaced by a new highway bridge, and the local county commission was trying to determine if it could stay in operation as a symbol of a bygone era. I had the unique opportunity to visit the site in 1988, talk with the ferry operator and develop a few sketches just months before it was permanently closed. The engine driving the ferry was a six-cylinder Chevrolet 250 mounted to the side of the ferry. It was exactly the same as the one in my first car.

Talking to the ferry operator, we learned that the ferry, although open twenty-four hours per day, would run less than half of the days per year due to high water, floods, extreme low water conditions, snags, floating logs and more.

Central Georgia

Our plan recommended that the ferry remain in operation as part of the historic Andersonville Trail in southwestern Georgia. The ferry was eventually donated to the Agricultural Museum located at Abraham Baldwin College in Tift County. The old ferry can still be seen sitting on blocks on the museum property.

A Scenic Georgia Sketchbook

The Spring House at Indian Springs State Park, Butts County

Indian Springs State Park claims to be the oldest state park in the United States. The flowing natural artesian springs have been used for centuries as drinking water and for their purported healing properties. Several treaties between the Creek Indian Nation and the State of Georgia were signed in the early 1800s. The First Treaty of Indian Springs was signed in 1821 and ceded thousands of acres of land, including Indian Springs, to the State of Georgia. A second treaty was signed in 1825 that secured adjacent lands held by the Creek Indian Chief William McIntosh. In 1826, the Treaty of Washington was signed and recognized by the U.S. government. After the signing of the treaties, the former Creek Indian lands were added to the State of Georgia. By this time, the springs were already popular, and a hotel had been developed near the present-day entrance to the state park, which is still standing today. The Georgia government set aside the land directly around the springs to be held in perpetuity as a public recreation area. As a result, Indian Springs is the oldest state-owned recreation area in the country. Indian Springs did not gain the title of "state park" until 1931, when it became one of the founding parks in the State of Georgia's new state park system (along with Vogel State Park). The oldest state park in the nation is Niagara Falls State Park in New York; it was established in 1885.

Many state parks date from the 1930s. More than eight hundred state parks were developed during the depression years under the work of the Civilian Conservation Corps (CCC) and the Works Progress Administration (WPA). Company 459 of the CCC came to Indian Springs and built many of the stone structures that surround the springs, including the spring house. The spring house was built over the spring. The original purpose of a spring house was to keep the spring water clean by excluding leaf debris and animals. The spring house was commonly enclosed and could also be used for refrigeration, as the cool waters kept the room temperature cool. The spring house at Indian Springs is still used by local residents to fill water jugs for home use.

4
NORTH GEORGIA

*Art is about sharing parts of yourself
that you can't share using words or other media.
—Emmie Huffman*

North Georgia contains some of the most beautiful mountains in the eastern United States. The Blue Ridge Mountains extend down into North Georgia, the Appalachian Trail begins in North Georgia and the headwaters for the Chattahoochee River begin in North Georgia. In addition to the mountains, North Georgia is home to some of the state's most important bodies of water, such as Lake Lanier, which is Atlanta's water supply; Lake Allatoona, which is Cobb County's water supply; and Lake Richard B. Russell, which forms a portion of the border with South Carolina. North Georgia was also the center of the Cherokee Nation and the point of beginning for the Trail of Tears as the Cherokee Indians were forced off their land and marched out to Oklahoma. The highest point in the state is located on Brasstown Bald amid the rhododendron. Tallulah Gorge State Park provides visitors with access to the deepest gorge in the eastern United States and was the location for the filming of the movie *Deliverance*.

North Georgia is also home to two of the state's most beautiful college campuses: the University of Georgia in Athens–Clarke County and Berry College in Rome. One of Georgia's most famous folk artists, Howard Finster, was also from North Georgia. Finster created his famous Paradise Gardens in Chattooga County.

North Georgia is as varied as the terrain is mountainous. It was hard not to include more sketches due to the overwhelming scenic beauty of the region.

Project Notes

In 1994, my firm was selected to master plan and design the first new state park in Georgia in more than forty years on three thousand acres of land that was going to be leased from Georgia Power Company around Tallulah Gorge and Tallulah Lake. At that time, the State of Georgia was pushing to build projects to capitalize on the tourism activity related to the upcoming 1996 Olympics. The current governor was Zell Miller, who grew up in North Georgia. Zell Miller was the first of several governors I have had the unique opportunity to work with during my career (the others are Governor Roy Barnes and Governor Nathan Deal). The biggest challenge for the project was the location of the visitor's center. The Georgia Department of Natural Resources under Commissioner Joe Tanner directed us to try to site the visitor's center in downtown Tallulah Falls as part of an economic development initiative to revitalize the small town. I struggled to make it fit on a small formerly commercial site and was frustrated that we were not considering the other three thousand acres around the gorge.

Two days before Christmas in 1994, I was making a presentation to Commissioner Tanner. He sensed my frustration and asked me where I thought the visitor's center should go. I quickly pointed to a spot on the north rim of the gorge. Commissioner Tanner asked for revised plans as soon as we could develop them. Working with architect Garland Reynolds from Hall County, we quickly redesigned the master plan. Today, the visitor's center is located on that spot on the north rim of the gorge.

List of Illustrations

67. Cast-Iron Arch, University of Georgia, Athens–Clarke County
68. Confederate Cemetery, Resaca, Gordon County
69. Abandoned Shops, Habersham County
70. Visitor's Center, Brasstown Bald, Union County

71. Olde Post Office, Georgia Marble Company, Nelson, Cherokee County
72. Richard B. Russell Dam, Elbert County
73. Dahlonega Gold Museum, Dahlonega, Lumpkin County
74. Manor House Ruins, Barnsley Gardens, Bartow County
75. Log Blockhouse, Fort Yargo State Park, Barrow County
76. Overshot Wheel, Berry College, Floyd County
77. The Ford Campus at Berry College, Floyd County
78. Chief Vann House State Historic Site, Murray County
79. The Printing Office at New Echota State Historic Site, Gordon County
80. Healan's-Head's Mill, Hall County
81. Wallace-Tatum Property, Forsyth County
82. Folk Art Church, Paradise Gardens, Chattooga County
83. Old Barn at Milam Farm, Cartersville, Bartow County

Cast-Iron Arch, University of Georgia, Athens–Clarke County

One of the most iconic pieces of Georgia history is the cast-iron Gateway Arch at the entrance to the North Campus of the University of Georgia. It is modeled after the Georgia State Seal and features the three pillars of "wisdom, justice and moderation." The Gateway Arch dates from the 1850s and was cobbled together from fence pieces that were used to keep livestock off the campus. The Arch served as the main entrance to the campus and originally could be closed by two iron gates. The downtown business district for the city of Athens lies directly across Broad Street from the Arch. I prepared a Campus Plan for the East Campus in the 1990s and have attended many functions on-campus. My daughter-in-law, Jennifer, is a graduate, and I have known many friends and colleagues who are UGA graduates.

The University of Georgia is the nation's first state university and was chartered by the Georgia legislature in 1785. The first president of the university was Abraham Baldwin. After holding classes in a log cabin, the oldest building on campus, now called "Old College," was built in 1806 and is a copy of Connecticut Hall at Yale University, which was Baldwin's alma mater. The university struggled in the early nineteenth century and by 1829 had an enrollment of only one hundred students. During the Civil War, the university was closed. The university facilities escaped unscathed

A Scenic Georgia Sketchbook

UNIVERSITY OF GEORGIA
CAST IRON ARCH
NORTH CAMPUS

from the war and reopened in 1866. More than one hundred students and alumni were killed in the war. The university became a land-grant college eligible for financial support from the federal government in 1872. By the late nineteenth century, the university had grown to include eighteen faculty and three hundred students. Explosive growth in the twentieth century has created a top-ranked university with 465 buildings on 762 acres (Athens Campus) and thirty-five thousand students.

North Georgia

CONFEDERATE CEMETERY, RESACA, GORDON COUNTY

I first visited this site when my firm was selected to prepare a master plan for the Resaca Civil War Battlefield in the mid-1990s. The Battle for Resaca was a major conflict in the Atlanta Campaign. Behind the walls of this cemetery are interred 450 Confederate soldiers killed during the two-day battle in May 1864. The burial ground was established in October 1866 on two and a half acres. There is a plaque on the stone wall placed by the United Daughters of the Confederacy. The stone wall was made by the Georgia School of Technology under the Works Progress Administration, probably dating the wall to the middle 1930s.

The Atlanta Campaign of the Civil War began with a series of battles as Sherman's army approached Atlanta from Chattanooga. The campaign began when Sherman's forces moved through Ringgold Gap on May 7, 1864. Generally, Sherman's forces followed the path of the Western and Atlantic Railroad that connected Chattanooga to Atlanta. Resaca was a small community on the Oostanaula River located approximately fifty miles south of Chattanooga. When Sherman approached, he found Confederate soldiers entrenched around a semicircle of hills surrounding the town with the river in their rear. The Federal troops assaulted along several points along the line. The Federal attacks allowed Sherman to secure artillery positions on high ground. These artillery positions could be directed at the railroad crossing over the river. Sherman also sent a column of troops to cross the river below Resaca. The Federal bombardment of the bridges and the flanking movement across the river forced the Confederates to retire and left Sherman in possession of Georgia north of the river.

Abandoned Shops, Habersham County

One of the most spectacular canyons in the eastern United States is Tallulah Gorge, which is two miles long and nearly one thousand feet deep. The gorge is considered one of the Seven Natural Wonders of Georgia. The gorge was cut through the mountainside by the Tallulah River. A hike down into the gorge includes crossing on a dramatic cable suspension bridge situated eighty feet above the floor of the gorge. There are a series of six waterfalls (known as Tallulah Falls) on the river that descend five hundred feet through the gorge before entering into Tugaloo Lake. The Jane Hurt Yarn Interpretive Center is located on the north rim of the gorge and includes exhibits on the flora and fauna as well as the history of the area.

In 1994, my firm was asked to design a new state park that became what is now the 2,689-acre Tallulah Gorge State Park. Prior to the state park,

Tallulah Gorge and the nearby city of Tallulah Falls were a well-known tourist stop on the way to western North Carolina. Many tourists stopped to take in the scenic beauty and discover the lure associated with the filming of the 1972 movie *Deliverance* in the gorge. The now abandoned Tallulah Falls Shortline Railroad crossed the gorge and was used by Disney in the filming of *The Great Locomotive Chase* in 1955. The gorge was also crossed on a high wire by the Great Wallenda in 1970. A dam was built upstream of the gorge by Georgia Power in 1913 to provide hydroelectric power to the growing city of Atlanta. The dam still collects and redirects water from Tallulah Falls Lake through a 6,666-foot tunnel around the falls to a generation station located 608 feet below the lake. Prior to the completion of the nearby state highway, tourist traffic passed these shops attempting to lure passersby. Today, the shops are empty, a victim of a bypass highway, but they still retain a charming eclectic roadside character.

Visitor's Center, Brasstown Bald, Union County

Brasstown Bald is the highest point in Georgia at an elevation of 4,784 feet above sea level. Brasstown Bald is part of the Blue Ridge Mountains and sits within the Chattahoochee-Oconee National Forest. There is a large parking area located approximately half a mile from the summit. There is a beautiful but strenuous trail to the summit that is surrounded by rhododendrons. When the rhododendrons are blooming in late spring and early summer, the hike to the summit is an absolute pleasure to behold.

The iconic observation tower was built in 1965. The first observation tower was built in 1935 by the CCC along with an improved lumber road to the summit. The tower facilities today include a visitor's center with a museum and a small theater. The view from the summit is spectacular, and visitors are able to see four states and the tall buildings in Atlanta on a clear day.

The area surrounding Brasstown Bald was originally settled by the Cherokee people. The mountain is known to the Cherokee natives as Enotah. The term *bald* refers to mountaintops in the southern Appalachians with an uninterrupted 360-degree view. The word *Brasstown* comes from a translation error by English-speaking settlers for the Cherokee word for their village.

A Scenic Georgia Sketchbook

The Chattahoochee-Oconee National forest features 867,000 acres across twenty-six counties and includes approximately 850 miles of trails. The forest is managed by the USDA Forest Service.

North Georgia

Old Post Office, Georgia Marble Company, Nelson, Cherokee County

Nelson is a small community originally built to support the Georgia Marble Company and quarry in Cherokee County/Pickens County. Many of the homes were part of the original company town. I was working in Nelson on the master plan for a small baseball park near downtown. I was told that this small shotgun building was originally used as the post office for the Georgia Marble Company. I have always been fascinated with shotgun homes. Although slightly rundown, this early 1900s example appeared generally intact.

Marble is synonymous with North Georgia. The Cherokee Indians used some marble in their crafts, but Henry Fitzsimmons, an Irish stonemason, is credited with spotting a marble outcrop in Pickens County along the Old Federal Road that crossed through the Cherokee lands in 1836. Quarrying of the marble for tombstones was begun around 1840 with deliveries by wagon. Samuel Tate purchased much of the land with the marble deposits in the 1830s through the Cherokee Land Lottery. The Tate, Atkinson Company began to quarry marble in 1850 primarily for tombstones. The quarry closed during the Civil War. The Georgia Marble Company was founded on May 10, 1884, by the Tate family. Branch railroads were added to connect the marble communities of Nelson and Tate to Marietta and Atlanta. By 1900, only Vermont produced more marble than Georgia. Some of the well-known buildings that use Georgia marble include the Georgia State Capitol, New York Stock Exchange, Library of Congress in Washington, D.C., the Federal Reserve Bank in Washington, D.C., the colossal statue of Lincoln in the Lincoln Memorial, the interior courtyards of the Supreme Court building and portions of the exterior of the east wing of the U.S. Capitol, along with the twenty-four exterior columns.

RICHARD B. RUSSELL DAM, ELBERT COUNTY

Richard B. Russell Dam is located approximated 50 miles north of Augusta on the Savannah River at the border with South Carolina. The dam was built between 1974 and 1985 by the U.S. Army Corps of Engineers. I was living in Augusta in 1984 and remember the press coverage associated with the opening of the dam. Full pool was reached in December 1984. The dam is 5,224 feet long. The concrete section of the dam spans 1,904 feet. The hydroelectric plant has a 600-megawatt capacity. I recently visited the dam as part of our master planning efforts for Bobby Brown State Park, which is located on a peninsula of land just below the dam.

Originally called Trotter Shoals Lake, it was renamed for Senator Richard Brevard Russell Jr., who was an adamant supporter of hydropower. The lake has 26,650 acres of water surface and approximately 540 miles of shoreline. The Russell Dam is a pump back, which pumps water upstream during the night when power demand is low from Lake Strom Thurmond and releases the water during the day and during times of peak demand. The Russell Dam is the largest USACE hydropower plant in the Southeast. Because the lake was built after 1974, there is no private use of the shoreline. The entire shoreline is undeveloped, with the exception of day use recreation areas and state parks.

Just below the dam is Bobby Brown State Park. During low water, the original footprint and some building ruins from the eighteenth- and nineteenth-century community of Petersburg is evident. Petersburg was a tobacco processing town with nearly 750 residents. Tobacco was shipped downstream on "Petersburg Boats." Cotton would eventually replace tobacco as a cash crop in Georgia, and Petersburg turned into a ghost town by the mid-1800s.

Dahlonega Gold Museum, Dahlonega, Lumpkin County

My wife Therese's firm, Signature Design, was hired to update the exhibits inside the Gold Museum. I had the opportunity to visit the old courthouse during the installation of the exhibits. I was able to crawl around the attic at that time. The exposed timbers in the attic were evidently pit-sawn based on the vertical saw blade marks. The old courthouse building dates from 1836 and is the oldest existing courthouse building in Georgia. The building was designed and built by Ephram Clayton and required two years to complete. The bricks were handmade from clay dug from nearby Cane Creek. The outer walls of the courthouse are solid brick and nearly twenty-four inches thick. According to the Georgia Department of Natural Resources, the bricks include trace amounts of gold.

Gold was discovered in the Dahlonega area in 1828 by Benjamin Parks while deer hunting. Within a year, thousands of miners moved to the area and created America's first major gold rush. The Cherokee Indians, still living on the land, were rounded up by federal troops and forcibly marched to Oklahoma. Congress approved Dahlonega as a location for a branch of the U.S. Mint in 1835. Dahlonega's mint stayed in operation until 1861. The name *Dahlonega* comes from the Cherokee word *dalanigei*, meaning "yellow money" or gold. After the outbreak of the Civil War, the mint closed. In 1871, the mint and associated land was donated to the newly created North Georgia Agricultural College, which is now the University of North Georgia. The Dahlonega branch of the mint had receipts during the first year of operation totaling $102,915. Until its last year of operation, receipts amounted to more than $6 million, including $1,378,719 worth of minted coins.

Manor House Ruins, Barnsley Gardens, Bartow County

The manor house was originally built in the 1850s by Godfrey Barnsley. Barnsley was a wealthy cotton and sea merchant originally born in Derbyshire, England. He settled in Savannah in the 1820s and married Julia Henrietta

Scarborough, the daughter of a prominent merchant family. By the late 1830s, Sir Godfrey Barnsley had become one of the wealthiest southern sea merchants. In 1839, he traveled north into the newly evacuated Cherokee Indian lands in northwest Georgia and was "overtaken" by the beauty of the region. In the 1840s, he assembled ten thousand acres and began building the estate, complete with an Italianate manor house and parterre gardens. The home featured hand-sculpted mantels, wall paneling, European antiques and modern plumbing with flushing commodes. The parterre garden was created with English boxwood, framing an intricate pattern of walkways. Julia Barnsley died in 1845 before the home was complete. During the Civil War, Union troops camped on the grounds. In 1864, Julia Bernard Barnsley (daughter of Godfrey and Julia) married Captain James Baltzelle and spent the rest of her life at the home and gardens. A storm struck the manor in 1906 and destroyed the roof. The family never rebuilt the home, and it fell into ruins. It was eventually purchased in the early 1990s. The ruins were stabilized, and the grounds developed as a golfing resort and spa.

BARNSLEY MANOR HOUSE RUINS

Log Blockhouse, Fort Yargo State Park, Barrow County

The log blockhouse at Fort Yargo State Park was built in 1793. The blockhouse was built to protect early settlers from Indian attacks. As many as thirty to fifty settlers took refuge within the one-room fort during Indian attacks. The blockhouse was moved to its current location in 2005 from a nearby site within the state park. The blockhouse resembles many of the log cabins built across the South. It is one-and-one-half stories tall, with front and back doors opposite to allow for air circulation during the warm summer days. The hand-hewn logs are notched with a half dovetail referred to as a chamber and notch. The spaces between the logs were originally chinked with straw or pieces of wood mixed with clay mortar. The roof is made from cedar shakes. Small firing holes or shooting ports were placed around the fort to provide a field of fire.

Fort Yargo State Park was dedicated in 1967 as part of the Marbury Creek Watershed project and includes 1,800 acres with recreational amenities surrounding a beautiful lake. I first worked at Fort Yargo State Park updating a master plan for Camp Will-a-way, which is a camp for children with disabilities.

North Georgia

OVERSHOT WHEEL, BERRY COLLEGE, FLOYD COUNTY

One of the most beautiful spots in Georgia, the Old Mill and Overshot Wheel were built in the 1930s by students at Berry College in order to produce cornmeal for the school. The iron hub in the wheel's center was donated to Berry College by the Republic Mining and Manufacturing Company following a request from Martha Berry. The wheel diameter is forty-two feet and considered one of the largest of this type in the nation. A reservoir on the campus provides the water to the wheel.

The Old Mill is dedicated to Henry Ford and M. Gordon Keown. Keown was a 1905 graduate of Berry College and spent his entire life associated with the school as a resident trustee and eventually as director. He played a major role in expansion of the campus from eighty-three acres to twenty-six thousand acres with help and support from Henry Ford.

Martha McChesney Berry was the daughter of Captain Thomas Berry, a veteran of the Mexican American War and the American Civil War, and Frances Margaret Rhea, a daughter of an Alabama planter. Her father was a partner in a wholesale grocery and cotton brokerage business in Rome. In 1871, Thomas Berry purchased Oak Hill, a 116-acre working farm. The

BERRY COLLEGE MILL

Oak Hill Greek Revival mansion was built in 1847 and was used by Union soldiers during the Atlanta Campaign of the Civil War. Thomas Berry purchased the home for $9,000. Martha Berry, who founded Berry College in 1902, began teaching Sunday school lessons from a log cabin playhouse on the Oak Hill Estate. When the cabin overflowed with students, a day school was established on what eventually became Berry College.

THE FORD CAMPUS AT BERRY COLLEGE, FLOYD COUNTY

Berry College was originally founded as the Boys Industrial School in 1902 by Martha Berry on eighty-three acres that she inherited from her father. The Martha Berry School for Girls was added in 1909. Martha Berry was the daughter of a wealthy Floyd County planter. She was sensitive to the impoverished condition of many of the people who lived in the area's mountains. She started by teaching Sunday school before developing the boarding school in 1902. From the beginning, the school accepted only students from rural areas. (This requirement was dropped in 1957.) Beginning in 1914, the students were required to work each week for eight hours. The work program helped to keep costs low, as students constructed campus facilities and provided maintenance. Martha Berry passed away in 1942, and the school struggled with declining enrollment. Ultimately, the college opened enrollment to qualified students from urban areas and commuters. Today, most of the students still continue to work on campus.

Martha Berry was a relentless fundraiser, seeking contributions from the nation's political and social elite. The buildings of the Ford campus were a gift from automobile manufacturer Henry Ford and completed in the 1920s. The architect for the breathtaking buildings was Harry Carlson from Boston.

Berry College is a private liberal arts college located a few miles north of Rome, Georgia. The Berry College campus consists of more than twenty-six thousand acres of land, making it the largest contiguous college campus in the world. Berry College has approximately 1,900 undergraduate students and 91 graduate students in four schools, including the Campbell Business School; the Carter School of Education and Human Sciences; the Evans School of Humanities, Arts, and Sciences; and the School of Mathematical and Natural Sciences.

Chief Vann House, State Historic Site, Murray County

The Chief Vann House is a state historic site operated and maintained by the Georgia Department of Natural Resources. The unusual house was built in 1804 and was the home of James Vann, the chief of the Cherokee Indian Nation. James was the son of a Scottish trader, Clement Vann, and his wife, a Cherokee chieftain's daughter. The brick home was part of a large farm and business operation that included slaves. James's son, Joseph, expanded the business and lived in the house until the Cherokee Indians were brutally expelled from Georgia as part of the Trail of Tears in 1834. A Georgia law was passed that made it illegal for Indians to employ white people. Because the property caretaker was a white man, Georgia confiscated the property. The Vann House was owned and lived in by numerous families until the mid-1940s. The home was purchased by the local community from Dr. J.E. Bradford in 1952 and given to the Georgia Historical Commission. The fully restored Vann House was dedicated in 1958 and is listed in the National Register of Historic Places.

A Scenic Georgia Sketchbook

Chief Vann House

The New Echota Treaty in 1835 relinquished Cherokee Indian claims to lands east of the Mississippi. Seven thousand federal and state troops were ordered into the Cherokee Nation to forcibly evict over fifteen thousand Cherokee Indians. Some escaped by boat, and others escaped into the mountains of North Carolina. The remaining thirteen thousand were rounded up and forced to leave by wagon, horse or on foot for an eight-hundred-mile route to eastern Oklahoma. As many as four thousand Cherokee Indians died of disease and starvation during the journey.

The Printing Office at New Echota State Historic Site, Gordon County

New Echota was the seat of local government and the capital of the Cherokee Nation established by the legislature in 1825. The Cherokee Council created a city with a series of streets and one hundred one-acre lots. Included among the government buildings was a council house, a supreme courthouse and the printing office.

North Georgia

The Cherokee Indians had developed their own alphabet and written language. Around 1809, a mixed-blood Cherokee named Sequoyah began developing a written form of the Cherokee language. By 1821, Sequoyah's syllable-based alphabet of eighty-six characters was complete and adopted by the Cherokee Council for use in their newspaper. The printing office was the home of the *Cherokee Phoenix* newspaper. Beginning in 1827, the print shop produced over 700,000 pages of broadsheets, religious tracts, government documents and newspapers. Ink was made from boiled linseed oil. During the six years of production, the print shop produced 260 issues of the newspaper. Major events covered by the newspaper included the Indian Removal Act of 1830 and actions by the State of Georgia to lay claim to the Cherokee lands. The paper's name was changed to the *Cherokee Phoenix and Indians' Advocate* to reflect the editor's interest in all things Native American. The bilingual newspaper was circulated throughout the Cherokee Nation and parts of the United States and Europe. Special printing type in both English and Cherokee alphabets was cast for use on the press.

The print shop building is a reconstruction of the original 1827 Phoenix Printing office.

THE PRINTING OFFICE @ NEW ECHOTA

Healan's-Head's Mill, Hall County

Healan's-Head's Mill was built in the 1850s. The gristmill is a two-and-one-half-story wood-frame structure with an overshot type waterwheel. It is located on the east bank of the North Oconee River. It was used primarily for grinding corn. The mill also served other agricultural uses, such as grinding wheat, shelling crops, sawmilling and, in the final years of use (1950s), producing lumber and roofing shingles. A primary feature of the mill is the twenty-eight-foot-diameter steel wheel, which replaced the original wheel in the 1930s. Water was diverted from a former mill pond along a metal flume to the overshot wheel. The mill underwent a remodel in the 1930s, which included the steel water wheel. The site also includes two other structures, which are believed to have served a number of purposes, one being a barn or corncrib, the other being a small mechanic shop or blacksmith shop. Healan's-Head's Mill was placed in the National Register of Historic Places in 1990. The mill is significant as an example of a mid-nineteenth-century rural industrial complex for processing agriculture products.

According to the National Register nomination form, there has been a mill on the site since 1852. In that year, Guilford Thompson sold an undivided half interest of a 70-acre tract to his brother-in-law, William Head. William Head was born in 1810 and married Sarah Thompson. After the purchase of the mill site in 1852, William Head became the miller. By 1860, William had expanded his land holdings to include 1,200 acres. In addition to grinding corn, his agricultural operations included raising swine, growing wheat and corn and raising a small number of livestock. He also grew peas, beans and sweet potatoes and churned 200 pounds of butter and 200 gallons of molasses. William Head passed away in 1889.

Wallace-Tatum Property, Forsyth County

The Wallace-Tatum property is located toward the northwestern corner of Forsyth County. The old barn was the only remnant still standing when my firm was hired to prepare a plan for a new community park on the property. The Wallace-Tatum property is located close to the Old Federal Road that originally passed through the Cherokee lands in North Georgia. The Old Federal Road was the first vehicular way and the earliest postal route west of the Chattahoochee River. Beginning to the east of the Hall County–Jackson County line, it linked Georgia and Tennessee across the Cherokee Nation. Prior to that time, the trace served as a trading path from Augusta to the Cherokees in northwest Georgia and southeast Tennessee. In 1803, the rights to use the route was agreed to in principle by the Cherokee Indian chiefs. The Treaty of Tellico established the Federal Road from the Chattahoochee

The barn on the Wallace-Tatum property, Forsyth County, Georgia.

River to Nashville. In 1820, regular stagecoach service was established along the route. In the 1820s and 1830s, the Old Federal Road became a major route to the gold fields near the Etowah River during Georgia's gold rush. Portions of the Old Federal Road were used to remove the Cherokee Indians as part of the Trail of Tears. With the development of railroads, the use of the Old Federal Road declined. By the 1850s, sections of the road had already been abandoned. By the early twentieth century, only a few sections remained in use. Portions of the Old Trace are visible near the Lawson Federal Highway in Pickens County.

I sketched the barn and presented prints to my client with the Parks and Recreation Department as a thank-you for giving us the work. I did not find the barn very unique architecturally, but I thought the simple lines and fencing in many ways were a great representation of a typical North Georgia barn and farm.

Folk Art Church, Paradise Gardens, Chattooga County

One of Georgia's most well-known and unique folk artists is Howard Finster. He called his home in Chattooga County Paradise Gardens. I visited the site for the first time in 2011 in preparation for a bid to do a master plan for his home and grounds. The majority of his art has been placed in storage by the estate or is on display in museums. However, the property is a life-size work of folk art and contains a unique collection of structures that were hand-built by Howard Finster. The center of the property contains the World Folk Art Church. I was unsure of the stability of the structure and therefore did not venture inside. The strange building was cobbled together with building parts and scraps much like most of his sculpture. I prepared the sketch and submitted it along with others as part of our unsuccessful bid for the master plan.

Howard Finster (1916–2001) was a Georgia folk artist and Baptist minister. He claimed to be inspired by God to spread the gospel through the design of his folk art sculpture garden and over forty-six thousand pieces of art. Howard Finster was one of thirteen children born to Samuel and Lula Finster in Valley Head, Alabama. He had only a sixth-grade education and claimed to have had his first vision when he was three years old. At that time, he saw his recently deceased sister Abbie Rose and she spoke to him and told him he would be a man of visions. Finster became a "born again" Christian at a Baptist revival at the age of thirteen and began to preach at age sixteen. He moved to Georgia in the 1940s. In 1961, he moved to what is now Paradise Gardens near Summerville. He began developing the gardens "to show all the wonderful things o'God's creation, kinda like the Garden of Eden." The Folk Art Church is five stories tall.

Old Barn at Milam Farm, Cartersville, Bartow County

This old barn was located on some high ground on the edge of Cartersville and near the Etowah River. The barn site was also very close to the Etowah Indian Mounds State Historic Site. I was retained to master plan the farm site for a future community park and trail along the Etowah River. The barn was going to be demolished as part of the park development. I sketched the barn to give as a gift to my client. I was drawn to the look of this barn because of the gambrel roof shape. In Georgia, a gambrel roof is not very common. The tattered metal gambrel roof, the typical shed additions on each side and the rambling wire fence create a classic image for the old farm.

The Etowah Indian Mounds were the site of a Native American Indian settlement from 1000 CE to 1550 CE. The site includes six earthen mounds representing the Mississippian Culture. The largest mound is sixty-three feet tall and was part of a ceremonial complex for ritual and burial of nobility. The Etowah site was designated a National Historic Landmark in 1964.

The Mississippian Culture was a mound-building Native American civilization that flourished in the Midwest and southeastern United States

Old Barn @
Milam Farm
Bartow County, Ga.

from approximately 800 CE to 1600 CE. The Mississippian civilization was composed of a series of urban settlements and satellite villages. The largest city was Cahokia, located in Illinois nearby St. Louis. Other Indian mound sites in Georgia include Kolomoki Mounds State Park in Early County and the Ocmulgee National Monument near Macon.

ACKNOWLEDGEMENTS

The content of this book would not have been possible without the support of a wide range of people, including my family, my former college professors, my former employers, my clients and many of the wonderful professionals I have had the opportunity to work with over the last thirty-six years. While I had the idea to create a similar book as a result of my first professional internship more than thirty-six years ago, it was the encouragement of my wife and children that provided the impetus to turn the original idea into reality.

My wife, Therese, has been a constant source of inspiration since we met. She is not only the love of my life, my best friend and my colleague but also a terrific designer and a great source for invaluable critiques of my work. My three children, Emmie, Russell and Raymond, have been a blessing and inspiration from the day they arrived in the world. They are all gifted artists. I feel like an amateur around them. Special thanks to my son Russell for encouraging and promoting my work with the development and maintenance of the website mygasketchbook.com.

Several professors at Auburn University molded my direction as a professional. Our program in the 1970s and early 1980s was heavily focused on providing students real-world experience with local governments in Alabama as our clients. I cannot say enough about Professors Richard Rome, Darrell Meyer and John Robinson. They created the Landscape

Acknowledgements

Acknowledgements

Architecture and Planning programs and contributed significantly to my love for small towns and historic preservation.

Professionally, I had the opportunity to be mentored by a few terrific professionals and managers. They all understood how to guide my efforts, led by example and importantly gave me enough encouragement to allow me to grow professionally while expanding our businesses. The first time I met Jim Cothran, FASLA, I knew we would work together very well. For sixteen years, we crisscrossed the state together providing professional services. He encouraged me in every way possible. I molded my future work with other firms based on his business model. We offered diverse services that included downtown planning, park planning, college campus planning, land use planning and urban design.

Professionally, I also want to thank Tom Bucci and Dave Goershel. Dave and Tom have managed to support all of my professional efforts for the last sixteen years with patience, careful guidance and terrific business acumen. They have acted as mentors, leaders and partners as we experimented with the creation of a planning and landscape architecture team in the firm. With their support, we grew the team and managed to survive various acquisitions that always made us stronger.

I have had the privilege of working with some excellent landscape architects and planners over the last thirty-seven years. I do not believe that we would have been as successful without my longtime partner and colleague, Lee Walton, AICP. Lee and I began working together twenty-four years ago. There have been quite a few highs and lows, but we managed to keep the candles burning and the work flowing. Our work together has taken us from small towns in Georgia to distant lands such as Afghanistan, Egypt and Great Britain. There is no one I could have imagined as a better partner and friend than Lee. Thank you, Lee.

I would be remiss if I did not mention a couple of other professionals who I have enjoyed working with, including Gregg Hudspeth (a great friend and photographer) and Michele Jamros. Gregg and Michele have successfully won their battles with cancer. They are a constant reminder to me of the importance of family and friends. A bad day at work is nothing compared to the battle between life and death. They both persevered and provide daily inspiration as an example of what we can overcome when we are determined to win.

As professionals, our careers are based on providing services to our clients. I am constantly amazed and thankful that I have had the opportunity to work with some loyal and appreciative clients, many of whom I have worked with

Acknowledgements

for more than twenty years. Without their continued support and willingness to keep sending work my way, there might not be *A Scenic Georgia Sketchbook*. I would especially like to thank Brian Bulthuis, the Honorable Tommy Allegood, James Albright, Brandon Douglas, Richard Crowdis, Michael McCoy, John Hudgens, Lequrica Gaskins, Judy McCorkle, Robert Eubanks, Tom Barber, the Honorable Jeff Reece, Congressman Ed Setzler; David Freedman, Paige Perkins, Kathy Brannon, Jimmy Gisi, Eddie Cannon and Randy Dowling.

I would also like to thank my dear next-door neighbors, Karen and David Daniell. I could not ask for better neighbors. They are kind, giving and very supportive of my work. David Daniell is a descendant of one of the early families in Cobb County. The Daniell Mill and the Concord Road Covered Bridge were built by his ancestors.

I would like to thank my brother, Bill, for editing and providing guidance with the manuscript for the book. He helped an artist and designer create credible text to support the sketches. His guidance was very much appreciated.

Most importantly I would like to thank my mom and dad, Miriam and Raymond, for an absolutely terrific childhood, loving family and patient guidance. I look back at the decisions we make that can have a profound effect on our life and I realize my parents were always there to help me make the right decision. My father taught me to be patient, hardworking, thoughtful and deliberate. My mother taught me to be kind, giving and unselfish. I think about them every day and draw from their lessons constantly. I wish dearly that I could see them again.

Thanks to everyone listed and unlisted. This book represents one person's love for the state of Georgia. *A Scenic Georgia Sketchbook* is for everyone who loves Georgia and can appreciate the beauty that surrounds us every day.

Appendix A
THE SEVEN NATURAL WONDERS OF GEORGIA

As listed in the *Georgia Voyager* magazine in 1997 and the *Atlanta Journal-Constitution* in 2001.

1. Radium Springs, Dougherty County
2. Tallulah Gorge, Rabun County
3. Okefenokee Swamp, Ware County and Charlton County
4. Warm Springs, Meriwether County
5. Amicalola Falls, Dawson County
6. Stone Mountain, DeKalb County
7. Providence Canyon, Stewart County

Appendix B
GEORGIA DURING THE CIVIL WAR

MEMBERS OF THE STAFF OF CONFEDERATE PRESIDENT JEFFERSON DAVIS FROM GEORGIA

Alexander H. Stephens, Vice President (Taliaferro County)
Robert Tombs, First Secretary of State (Wilkes County)
Philip Clayton, Secretary of the Treasury
John Archibald Campbell, Assistant Secretary of War (Wilkes County)
Alexander Robert Lawton, Quartermaster General of the Confederate States (Jenkins County)
Isaac Munroe St. John, Commissary General
William H. Brown, Assistant Secretary of State

TIMELINE OF EVENTS AND ENGAGEMENTS DURING THE CIVIL WAR IN GEORGIA

1862	The Great Locomotive Chase (Kennesaw)
1862	Siege of Fort Pulaski (Chatham County)
September 1863	The Battle of Chickamauga (Catoosa County and Walker County)

Appendix B

February 1864	Federal invasion of Georgia; skirmishing around Dalton (Whitfield County); Andersonville prisoner of war camp established
May–September 1864	The Atlanta Campaign
May 7–13, 1864	Battle at Rocky Face Ridge (Whitfield County)
May 13–15, 1864	Battle of Resaca (Gordon County)
May 17, 1864	Battle of Adairsville (Bartow County)
May 25, 1864	Battle of New Hope Church (Paulding County)
May 27, 1864	Battle at Pickett's Mill (Paulding County)
June 15–18, 1864	Lot Mountain–Pine Mountain–Brushy Mountain Line (Cobb County)
June 22, 1864	Battle at Kolb's Farm (Cobb County)
June 27, 1864	Battle at Kennesaw Mountain (Cobb County)
July 2, 1864	Battle at Ruff's Mill (Cobb County)
July 20, 1864	Battle of Peachtree Creek (Fulton County)
July 22, 1864	Battle of Atlanta (Fulton County)
July 28, 1864	Battle of Ezra Church (Fulton County)
August 6, 1864	Battle at Utoy Creek (Fulton County)
August 14, 1864	Battle at Dalton (Whitfield County)
August 20, 1864	Battle at Lovejoy's Station (Clayton County)
August 31–September 1, 1864	Battle of Jonesboro (Clayton County)
October 1864	Battle of Allatoona Pass (Bartow County)
November 1864	Burning of Atlanta (Fulton County)
November 15–December 22, 1864	Sherman's March to the Sea

Appendix B

December 13, 1864	Capture of Fort McAllister (Bryan County)
April 1865	Robert E. Lee surrenders at Appomattox, Virginia
April 26, 1865	General Joseph E. Johnston surrenders at Durham Station, North Carolina
May 1865	Andersonville POW camp is liberated
May 10, 1865	President Jefferson Davis captured near Irwinville, Georgia (Irwin County)

Appendix C
OUTLINE OF GEORGIA HISTORY TO 1861

1540	Hernando de Soto leads an exploration through Georgia
1570	Spanish establish Franciscan missions along the coast on Sapelo Island, St. Simons Island and Cumberland Island
1670	Establishment of Charles Town and the new English colony of South Carolina
1721	Fort King Georgia is established near the mouth of the Altamaha River (abandoned in 1727)
1733	General James Edward Oglethorpe lands at Yamacraw Bluff (Savannah) on February 12 with plans to build a town and establish a royal colony under King George.
1738	Fort Frederica is established on St. Simons Island
1739	War of Jenkins Ear—Oglethorpe assaults the Spanish stronghold at St. Augustine but is not successful and withdraws in 1740
1742	Battle at Bloody Marsh, the Spanish are defeated near the south end of St. Simons Island
1755	Population of the Georgia colony includes 4,500 white and 1,850 Black residents

Appendix C

1760	Georgia population grows to 10,000 (one-third slaves)
1773	Georgia population is 33,000, including 15,000 slaves
April 1775	American Revolutionary War erupts with a battle at Lexington and Concord, Massachusetts
1776	On August 2, Georgia's three congressional delegates—George Walton, Button Gwinnett and Lyman Hall—sign the Declaration of Independence
1777	Georgia adopts the first state constitution
1777	Georgia establishes the first eight counties, including Chatham, Richmond, Glynn, Effingham, Camden, Burke, Wilkes and Liberty
December 1778	British forces under General Augustine Provost and Colonel Archibald Campbell capture and occupy Savannah
1779	Augusta falls to the British
February 1779	Battle of Kettle Creek, Elijah Clark leads Georgia Militia to victory over the British in Wilkes County
1779	Battle of Savannah, unsuccessful attempt by Franco-American forces to retake Savannah results in a loss of 750 allies
1780–1781	Augusta is recaptured. The capital moves to Augusta
1781	British surrender at Yorktown, Virginia
1782	British evacuate Savannah
1783	September 3. The Treaty of Paris is signed by representatives of King George III and of the United States, ending the American Revolutionary War
1787	The U.S. Constitution is signed in Philadelphia
January 2, 1788	Georgia is the fourth state to ratify the Constitution

Appendix C

May 1789	Georgia ratifies a new state constitution.
1790	The first U.S. Census records Georgia's population as 82,548
1794	Eli Whitney receives a patent for the cotton gin
1800	The Georgia population has grown to 162,000. There are approximately 35,000 Native Americans in Georgia. Primarily Creek in the south and west and Cherokee in the north.
1804	The state capital is moved from Louisville to Milledgeville
1812–15	The War of 1812 is fought between the United States and the United Kingdom
1814	General Andrew Jackson, with assistance from 900 Georgia militia, defeats the Creek in the Battle of Horseshoe Bend
1828	Gold is discovered in Dahlonega
1838	General Winfield Scott occupies Cherokee lands and forces the Cherokee on the Trail of Tears to the Oklahoma Territory.
1840s	Railroad expansion includes the Western & Atlantic Railroad, which converges with two other railroads in Terminus, later named Marthasville (named for Martha Lumpkin, daughter of the Georgia governor) and in 1845 renamed Atlanta
1840	Georgia population includes 408,000 white and 284,000 Black residents
1843	The Central of Georgia Railroad completed, linking Savannah to Macon
1844–46	Mexican American War
1846	Macon & Western Railroad completed, linking Atlanta and Macon
1850	Compromise of 1850 approved in Congress
1851	Western & Atlantic Railroad completed between Chattanooga, Tennessee, and Atlanta

Appendix C

1853	Atlanta & West Point Railroad is completed
1859	Georgia produces 701,840 bales of cotton
1860	Georgia population increases to 592,000 white and 466,000 Black people. Abraham Lincoln is elected president of the United States
December 20, 1860	South Carolina is the first state to secede from the Union
January 2, 1861	Georgia secedes from the Union

Appendix D
GEORGIA'S CAPITAL CITIES

1777–1780
Savannah

1780–1795
Augusta

1795–1804
Louisville

1804–1868
Milledgeville

1868–PRESENT
Atlanta

Appendix E
SKETCH LOCATOR

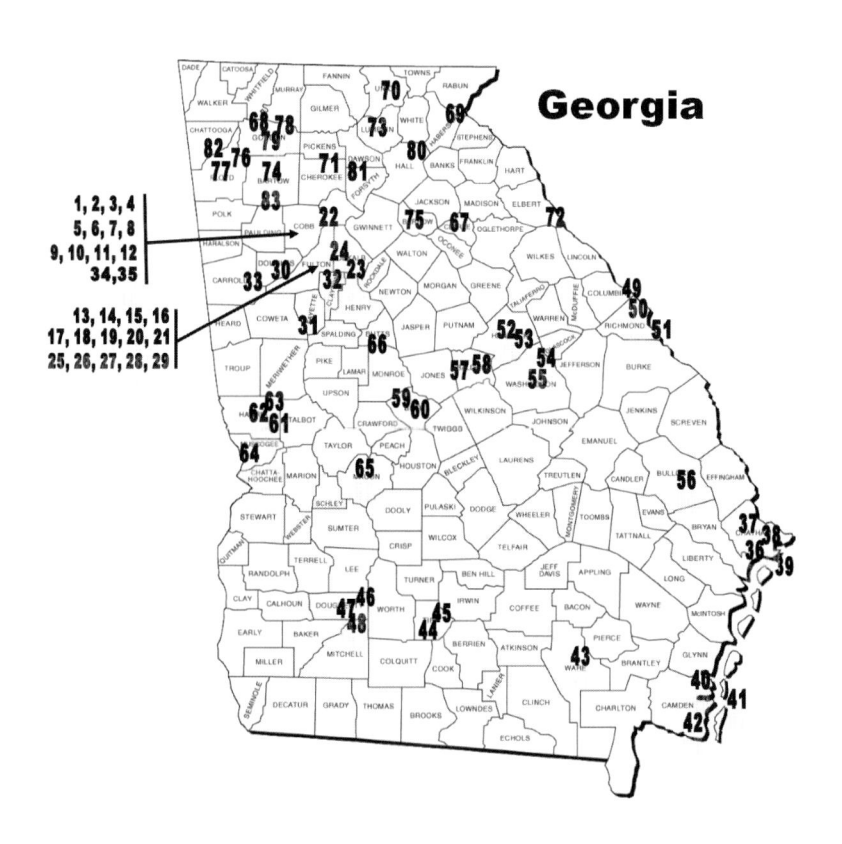

Georgia

1, 2, 3, 4
5, 6, 7, 8
9, 10, 11, 12
34, 35

13, 14, 15, 16
17, 18, 19, 20, 21
25, 26, 27, 28, 29

BIBLIOGRAPHY

Books and Periodicals

Atlanta Campaign Heritage Trail. Georgia's Civil War Heritage Trails Inc., 2004.

Atlanta's Lasting Landmarks. Atlanta Urban Design Commission, 1987.

Baumgartner, Richard A., and Larry M. Strayer. *Kennesaw Mountain, June 1864: Bitter Standoff at the Gibraltar of Georgia.* Huntington, WV: Blue Acorn Press, 1998.

Blumenson, J.G. *Identifying American Architecture, A Pictorial Guide to Styles and Terms, 1600–1945.* New York: American Association of State and Local History, 1977, 1981.

Boney, F.N. *A Walking Tour of the University of Georgia.* Athens: University of Georgia Press, 1989.

Byrd, Beth Wheeler. *Hyde Farm Cultural Landscape Report.* Atlanta: National Park Service, Southeast Regional Office, 2012.

Carver, Kaye, and Myra Queen, eds. *Memories of a Mountain Shortline: The Story of the Tallulah Falls Railroad.* Rabun Gap, GA: Foxfire Press, 1976.

Cashin, Edward J. *The Brightest Arm of the Savannah: The Augusta Canal 1845–2000.* Augusta, GA: Augusta Canal Authority, 2002.

Coker, Clent. *Barnsley Gardens at Woodlands: The Illustrious Dream.* Atlanta: Julia Publishing Company, 2000.

Coleman, Johnie. *Centennial Book in Commemoration of the Civil War.* Hewett Publishers, 1961.

Bibliography

Georgia Civil War Commission and Department of Industry, Trade and Tourism. *Crossroads of Conflict. A Guide for Touring Civil War Sites in Georgia.* Atlanta: Georgia Department of Natural Resources, 1993.

Georgia Historical Society. *Georgia, A State History.* Charleston, SC: Arcadia Publishing, 2003.

Gibson, Dorothy. *Jekyll Island's Historical Heritage, The Millionaire's Era in Pictures.* Mary T. Griffith Publication, 1970.

Horn, Stanley F. *The Campaign for Atlanta.* Eastern Acorn Press, 1986.

Howell, Shepard L. "Landscapes of the Past." *Georgia Backroads,* Summer 2019.

Installation Design Guidelines, Fort Gillem, Georgia. Robert and Company, 1989.

Installation Design Guidelines Fort McPherson, Georgia. Robert and Company, 1989.

Kent, Leland. *Abandoned Georgia: Traveling the Backroads.* Charleston, SC: Arcadia Publishing, 2019.

Kirby, Joe. *The Lockheed Plant.* Charleston, SC: Arcadia Publishing, 2011.

Kovarik, Joseph. *Vanishing Landmarks of Georgia, Gristmills and Covered Bridges.* Winston-Salem, NC: John F. Blair, 2016.

Lawson, Sherron D. *A Guide to the Historic Mill Town of Roswell, Georgia.* Roswell, GA: Roswell Historical Society, 1996.

Linley, John. *The Georgia Catalog, Historic American Buildings Survey: A Guide to the Architecture of the State.* Athens: University of Georgia Press, 1982.

March to the Sea Heritage Trail. Georgia's Civil War Heritage Trails Inc., 2003.

Martin, Clarece. *A Glimpse of the Past. A History of Bulloch Hall and Roswell, Georgia.* Roswell, GA: Lake Publications, 1973, 1987.

McCaig, Barbara, and Chris Boyce. *Georgia State Park Guide.* Wauwatosa, WI: Affordable Adventures, 1988.

Roth, Darlene R., PhD. *Architecture, Archaeology and Landscapes: Resources for Historic Preservation in Unincorporated Cobb County Georgia.* Marietta, GA: Cobb County Historic Preservation Commission, 1988.

Russell, Lisa M. *Lost Towns of North Georgia.* Charleston, SC: The History Press, 2016.

———. *Underwater Ghost Towns of North Georgia.* Charleston, SC: The History Press, 2018.

Scaife, William R. *The Atlanta Campaign: A Guide to the Atlanta Campaign.* Dalton, GA: Dalton-Whitfield Chamber of Commerce, 2000.

Scruggs, Carroll Proctor. *Georgia Historical Markers, The Completed Texts of 1752 Markers.* Bay Tree Grove, 1973.

Bibliography

Sears, Joan Niles. *The First One Hundred Years of Town Planning in Georgia.* Atlanta: Cherokee Publishing Company, 1979.

Secrist, Philip L. *The Battle of Resaca: Atlanta Campaign, 1864.* Macon, GA: Mercer University Press, 1998.

Temple, Sarah Blackwell Gober. *The First Hundred Years. A Short History of Cobb County, in Georgia.* Walter W. Brown Publishing Company, 1935.

Wiggins, Dr. David N. *Georgia's Confederate Monuments and Cemeteries.* Charleston, SC: Arcadia Publishing, 2006.

Williams, Clara Daniell. *Daniel Family History, Book Two.* WH Wolfe Associates Historical Publications, 1992.

Yates, Bowling C. *Historic Highlights in Cobb County.* Marietta, GA: Cobb Landmarks and Historical Society, 2001.

ABOUT THE AUTHOR

Ronald R. Huffman is a practicing landscape architect, community planner and historian who has been practicing in Georgia for more than thirty-six years. He holds multiple degrees from Auburn University, including a bachelor's degree in landscape architecture and a master's in community planning from the School of Architecture and Fine Arts and a master's in history with a concentration in historic preservation from the College of Liberal Arts. He has served as an adjunct professor to the School of Architecture at Southern Polytechnic State University, where he taught classes in environmental planning and landscape architecture. He is also a past president of the Georgia Chapter of the American Society of Landscape Architects.

His professional career has focused on providing high-quality design, planning and historic preservation services to communities all across Georgia, the Southeast and recently the Midwest. His favorite projects include the design and development of gardens around Radium Springs in Albany, Georgia; the Heritage Park and Silver Comet Trail in Cobb County, Georgia; Tallulah Gorge State Park in Rabun County, Georgia; the rebuilding of Johnsons Shut-ins State Park in Missouri; the Emiquon Preserve in Illinois; the park systems in Acworth, Kennesaw, Forsyth County

About the Author

and Chamblee, Georgia; the streetscapes in Montezuma, Clarkston and Sandersville, Georgia; the landscape renovation at the Woodrow Wilson House in Augusta, Georgia; and the renovation of Plant Park in Waycross. He also thoroughly enjoyed master planning the expansion of the University of Georgia campus and being part of the master planning team that helped to prepare Stone Mountain Park for the 1996 Olympics.

He is a self-taught, part-time artist who has deep southern roots that go back to the antebellum South in north Alabama and Hancock County, Georgia. He sees art in the history that surrounds us and enjoys drawing these unique treasures. He has always enjoyed the fine art and craft of pencil drawing. He also enjoys bringing attention to sometimes forgotten pieces of history and interpreting what he sees with nothing more than a pencil.

Visit us at
www.historypress.com